UNDERSTANDING INDONESIA

For Raymond Firth,
mahaguru

Understanding Indonesia

Edited by
LESLIE PALMIER

Gower

Published by
Gower Publishing Company Limited,
Gower House, Croft Road, Aldershot, Hampshire, England.

and

Gower Publishing Company,
Old Post Road,
Brookfield,
Vermont 05036,
U.S.A.

British Library Cataloguing in Publication Data

Understanding Indonesia.
   1. Indonesia——Social conditions
   I. Palmier, Leslie
   959.8'038   HN703.5

Library of Congress Cataloging in Publication Data

Understanding Indonesia.

   Bibliography: p.
   1. Indonesia   I. Palmier, Leslie H.
DS615.U54 1985   959.8   84-21133

ISBN 0-566-00784-3

Printed and bound in Great Britain by
Antony Rowe Limited, Chippenham, Wilts.

Contents

Our thanks to Oxford University Press for permission to reproduce Figures 1 and 2 from Ooi, Jin-Bee, *The Petroleum Resources of Indonesia*, Kuala Lumpar, 1982

Authors

HARVEY DEMAINE is Lecturer in Geography with reference to
South East Asia at the School of Oriental and African Studies,
University of London. His research interests in the region
began in 1970 when he was attached to a project on irrigated
agriculture in Thailand under the auspices of the Mekong
Committee. His subsequent work and publications have been
mainly concerned with agricultural development problems in
Thailand and Burma. From 1976 he has taken an interest in
Indonesia, principally in agricultural development, food
production and settlement planning. Dr. Demaine's recent
publications include:

(With Ng, R. C. Y. and Dixon, C. J.) 'Land use and socio-
economic changes under the impact of irrigation in the Lam
Pao project area in Thailand', *Final Report of the SOAS
Lam Pao Land Use Research Project for the Mekong Committee,*
London 1978.
'Burma: problems of agricultural development planning' in
Southeast Asian Affairs 1978, London 1978.
'Furnivall reconsidered:plural societies in South East Asia
in the post-colonial era' in Clarke, C. G., Ley, D. F. and
Peach, G. C. K. (eds.) *Geography and Ethnic Pluralism,*
London 1984.

ANGELA HOBART teaches at Goldsmith's College, University of
London. She first took an interest in Indonesia in the 1970s,
with field work in Bali for a PhD. Several return visits
have followed, with continued research on art, theatre and
ritual. The British Academy helped finance her most recent
trip, in 1979-80. Some of Dr. Hobart's writings are:

'Protagonists in the Parwas: the mystical and genealogical
  genesis of confrontation in Balinese literature' in
  Pengkajian Budaya, Bali 1981.
'The dance of the shadows: teachings of a poet-priest' in
  Lang, B. (ed.) *The Dancing Word; Aspects of Intellectual
  Rituals in World Religions*, Munich 1984 (in German).
'The noble, the base, the comic: the shadow play and operetta
  as mediums of education in Bali' in *Colloquium Volume on
  Ethno - Perspectives in Cognitive Development*, London forth-
  coming 1985.
'Creativity in Balinese theatre' in *Colloquium Volume on
  Malay and Indonesian Studies*, Leiden forthcoming 1985.

*The Balinese Shadow Play Figures: Their Ritual and Social
  Significance*, London forthcoming 1985.

MICHAEL LEIFER is Reader in International Relations at the
London School of Economics and Political Science. He takes a
special interest in South East Asia including Indonesia,
where he has been a frequent visitor. His publications
dealing specifically with Indonesia are:

Malacca, Singapore and Indonesia, Netherlands 1978.
Indonesian Foreign Policy, London 1983.

LESLIE PALMIER is Reader in Sociology and Director of the
Centre for Development Studies at the University of Bath,
as well as Associate Fellow of St. Antony's College, Oxford.
He first went to Indonesia in the early 1950s to undertake
field-work in Java; several return visits have followed.
He has published:

Social Status and Power in Java, London 1960, 1969.
Indonesia and the Dutch, London 1962.
Indonesia, London 1965.
Communists in Indonesia, London 1974.
The Control of Bureaucratic Corruption: Case Studies in Asia,
  New Delhi 1984.

JOHN WALTON has been Lecturer in South-East Asian Economics, Centre for South-East Asian Studies, at the University of Hull since 1970. He visited Indonesia in 1974 and has published:

'Development of the petroleum industry in Sumatra' *Sumatra Research Bulletin,* May 1974.

Preface

The papers offered here, apart from the Introduction, are
revised versions of lectures given at a conference of the
same title, 'Understanding Indonesia', held under the auspices
of the Asian Studies Centre, St. Anthony's College, Oxford,
in April 1983. Addressed primarily to those who may know
a little about Indonesia and wish to know more, they try
not only to analyse events and situations in that country,
but also to show the perspectives of Indonesians themselves.

I am most grateful to my fellow-authors for generously
agreeing to revise their papers for publication, to Mr.David
Young of Oxford Analytica, Ltd., for financial assistance
towards the preparation of the papers, and to Elizabeth
Sherrard of Bath University for typing the script ready
for the camera.

Bath, August 1984   Leslie Palmier

Republic of Indonesia

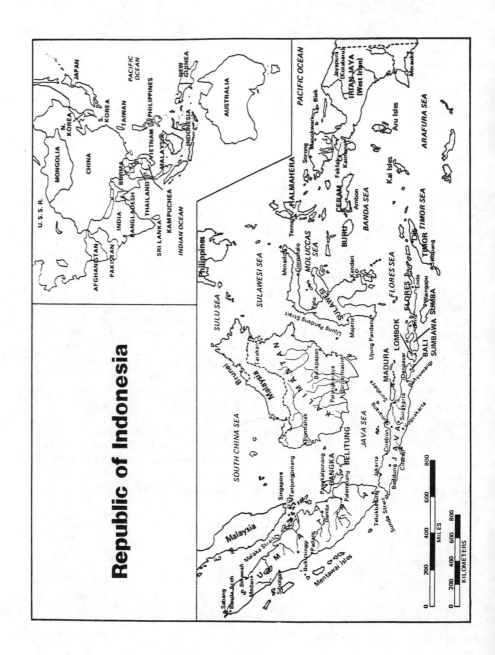

1 Introduction

LESLIE PALMIER

Indonesia forms part of the world's largest archipelago which
lies between Malaysia and the Philippines to the north and
Australia to the south. From northern Sumatra in the West
to Irian Jaya in the east runs a distance of nearly 3,200
miles. This is further than from the west of Ireland to the
Caspian Sea, and as far as from the west coast of the United
States to Bermuda in the Atlantic. Its land area totals
some 735,000 square miles, or about a quarter that of the
United States. The five largest islands in the archipelago
are (in decreasing order of size): Kalimantan (where Sarawak
and Sabah form part of Malaysia, and Brunei is newly independent), Sumatra, Irian Jaya (the eastern half of the island
is Papua New Guinea), Sulawesi, and Java. There are in
addition some 13,700 islands, of which it is thought that
6,000 are inhabited. Lying across the equator, Indonesia
enjoys a tropical climate with only slight seasonal changes.

   The 1980 Census reported a population of 148 million, but
it is generally considered that this is too low, and that
the current numbers are in the region of 160 million. The
population, however, is very unevenly distributed, with nearly
two thirds living on the smallest of the islands listed above,
namely Java, which with its very small neighbours Madura and
Bali accounts for only 7 per cent of the land area. This
concentration is a result of the fertile nature of its
volcanic soil, and ready access from north to south, which

1

have encouraged more intensive cultivation and development.

Depending on to whom he is speaking, an Indonesian will
identify himself usually first by his village, then his
ethnic group, and lastly, when meeting a foreigner, his
country. It is therefore important to bear in mind that the
view that an Indonesian takes of his country is affected by
the place of his ethnic group in the scheme of things. There
are some 300 such groups, differing considerably in size. No
account has been taken of ethnic origin since the 1930 Census,
so one is compelled to rely on that enumeration to estimate
the proportions of each ethnic group in the population.
Though it is unlikely that the larger differences have been
substantially reduced, the same may not be true for the
smaller. With this caution, then, one may report that the
larger groups were the Javanese, whose homelands are in
Central and East Java, and who accounted for 45 per cent of
the population; the Sundanese of West Java, 14 per cent; the
Madurese and the Coastal Malays, each 8 per cent, the
Makassarese-Buginese of south Sulawesi, 4 per cent; the
Menangkabau of west Sumatra, 3 per cent; the Balinese, the
Batak and the Acehnese (pr. Achehnese), both of north
Sumatra, each accounting for between 1 and 2 per cent. Size
is, of course, no reliable indicator of importance. Though
the large numbers of Javanese have inevitably given their
stamp to much of Indonesian life, the Batak and Menangkabau,
for example, have made contributions out of all proportion
to their minute fractions of the population. These ethnic
groups, with the exception of the Papuans, are all of Malay
stock. Though there are similarities between their customs
and languages (these total some 365), members of each group
are aware of their distinctive characteristics; for instance
that a Javanese differs from a Sundanese, and he in turn from
a Batak. Of course, in the present day, many forces are at
work to unify the various peoples. In particular, the
national language, Indonesian, is rapidly coming into widespread use.

Though, or perhaps because, they live on islands, the
Indonesian peoples have hardly been insular, but have been
perpetually exposed to the currents of change. Two thousand
years ago they still lived in small communities, relatively
democratic in character, devoted to rice-growing or fishing.
Despite their division into tribes and ethnic groups, their
levels of civilisation were probably similar, and characterised
by animistic beliefs. Then, about the first century AD, we
hear of seven kingdoms, probably rulers exerting some kind of
personal authority over a vaguely defined area and a number

of settlements.

In the third century merchants and priests from southern
India brought Indian civilisation to the islands. The
original travellers were disciples of Hinduism; from the
fifth century onwards they were joined by Buddhists. In time,
in South East Asia the two religions merged into Hindu-
Buddhism. Both contributed to the formation of Indonesian
principalities between the fifth and seventh centuries.

Beginning with the seventh century, powerful kingdoms arose.
A Buddhist dynasty known as Shrivijaya maintained a sea-
based empire from the south of Sumatra. In Java, Hindu
rulers held sway and built the temples to be seen on the
Dieng plateau in the central part of the island. There too,
their successors, Buddhists, erected the greatest of all
monuments in the archipelago, the Borobudur. In turn, they
were displaced by the Hindu state of Mataram, which built the
temple complex at Prambaban. This dynasty in course of time
grew strong enough to destroy Shrivijaya and to control the
whole of the island. It was nevertheless supplanted by the
greatest of the Javanese empires, Mojopahit, which held sway
for most of the fourteenth century.

Islam began infiltrating the archipelago from the end of the
thirteenth century, brought by, again, Indian merchants,
though now from Gujerat rather than southern India. In the
next century the religion had gathered enough strength to
give rise to several new states, most prominent among them
being the empire of Malacca, on the Malay peninsula. In
Java, some of the coastal principalities were ruled by
Muslims, others by Hindu-Buddhists. Mojopahit, now much
reduced, fell before a coalition of Muslim princes between
1513 and 1528. The end of the strongest Hindu-Buddhist state
meant that in due course Islam became the established religion
in the islands (as well as the Malay peninsula); one most
important exception was Bali, which to this day has remained
true to its Hindu traditions. However, this did not mean
that in Java the new converts abandoned the Hindu-Buddhism
they had followed for a thousand years or more. On the
contrary, just as they had not jettisoned their animism when
they accepted Indian civilisation, so now they added Islam
as a further layer of belief and practice. As Dr. Hobart
recounts below, the shadow-play, based on the Hindu epics,
continued to be performed and supported. It is perhaps not
without interest that the present-day Javanese elite look
back to Hindu-Buddhist Mojopahit as the embodiment of Javanese
greatness, not to the later Muslim Mataram, though that, as

we shall see, was also a very important power in its day.

The people of the islands now had to learn to cope with strangers from even further away than India; the Portuguese had arrived in search of spices, as part of their war against the Muslims, whom they called Moors, and their mission to convert the heathen to Christianity. Spices came mainly from the Moluccas, a group of small islands lying between present-day Sulawesi and Irian Barat. The Portuguese took Malacca in 1511, and proceeded to drive their Muslim competitors from the seas. For a time they were the predominant power in the archipelago. There were also, however, several important Muslim states, Aceh in north Sumatra, Mataram and Demak in Java, Ternate and Tidore in the Moluccas. Together they managed to contain, but not to expel, the Portuguese; indeed Ternate gave them the monopoly of the clove trade. The Portuguese nemesis was to lie at the hands of other Europeans, namely the Dutch, whose East India Company's ships entered Indonesian waters at the end of the century.

The Dutch differed from the Portuguese in many ways; one of the most important was that they had little interest in either fighting Islam as such, or in converting the heathen to Christianity; their sole concern was in profitable trade. To do so they drove the Portuguese from the Moluccas, and already by 1605 Amboina had recognised their suzerainety. They became the dominant power there when, as the least evil compared with the Spaniards or the Portuguese, Ternate chose them. Not so with the new power which arose at Makassar further west; after a visit by both Dutch and Portuguese, it opted for Islam! It remained an independent centre of trade, dealing with European traders of many nationalities, until 1667. At the other end of the archipelago, Aceh's aspirations to dominance were crushed by a coalition between Portuguese Malacca and two Islamic states of the peninsula. Meanwhile, Java was the theatre of frequent warfare between the inland Islamic Javanese state of Mataram, the Hinduised Balinese in the east, and the Islamic Sundanese port-state of Bantam in the west.

The Dutch had now concluded that since 'the countries of Asia exceed those of Europe in population, consumption of goods and industry', there was little demand for products from Europe. They therefore limited their trading activities to Asia, instead of between Asia and Europe, and sent the profits to Europe in a very few cargoes of extremely high value. 'Trade' implied, of course, on terms imposed by the Company. There was no intention of obtaining territory; they

4

used their superior seamanship and armament to apply a
monopoly control of maritime trade. Having established their
centre at Batavia on Java, they acquired mastery of the Java
sea and broke the power of Mataram. However, it remained
sovereign, as were Bantam, Aceh, and Makassar. With the fall
of Malacca in 1641, the Dutch company had no rival in the
Indonesian seas, and reached its zenith. It controlled all
the shipping lanes from the Bay of Bengal to Japan, with its
own trading posts on the way; it held Formosa (now called
(Taiwan), most of Ceylon, and established a relay station
which later became Cape Town. All this had been accomplished
at the expense of much blood and suffering, not only of the
competitors with the Dutch, but also of the local people.
Those of the Moluccas were reduced to misery, ruin, and
bondage to ensure a monopoly of spices for the Company;
indeed the population of Banda was virtually exterminated.

For the next two centuries the Dutch dominated the Asian
shipping-lanes to their great profit, and to the ruin of
local trade. The local states disintegrated and fell under
the Company's sway. Though it sought to avoid territorial
acquisitions, preferring simply to have local rulers acknowledge its sovereignty, it found this impossible. From 1705,
when it acquired complete overlordship of West Java, until
1941 the Company controlled events in the Indies from
Batavia.

About this time the Dutch faced an economic crisis, as
the profits from inter-Asian trade were falling; they were
rescued by the successful transplantation to West Java of the
coffee tree from South India. To this crop the Company
applied the same policy as it had to spices, compelling
cultivators to produce at its own prices, so little or no
benefit accrued to them.

Mataram had now become an economic dependency. Quarrels over
the succession, in which the Company intervened to its advantage, ensured that by 1755 the once proud empire had been
reduced to two small princely states, Jogyakarta and Surakarta.
They, like two others (Bantam and Ceribon) were vassals of
the Company; the rest of Java was directly governed. The one
good thing to be said for the Company's assumption of territorial power is that for the first time in a very long while,
peace reigned in Java.

The costs of empire, as well as of maladministration,
pushed the Company into bankruptcy, and in 1796 it was taken
over by the Dutch government. Matters did not improve for

the people of the islands. Land - with the people on it -
was sold to European planters. Thousands perished, at the
time of the Napoleonic wars, in the building of a defensive
road running from east to west along the north coast of the
island. This did not prevent the English East India Company
taking the island in 1811, installing Raffles as Governor-
General. His tenure was brief, if notable; he centralised
the government of Java more than ever before, and introduced
direct taxes on land. As part of a general settlement the
island was returned to the Netherlands in 1816.

Hardly had the Dutch re-organised the administration, when
they found, in 1825, that a disputed succession in Jogyakarta
developed into a revolt against their rule. This became known
as the Java War; and it took five years, several thousand
lives, and a guarantee of tenure to the Javanese nobility who
remained loyal, for the Dutch to gain the upper hand. This
was not the end of their troubles. In Europe, Belgium, then
a part of the Netherlands, rebelled and seceded. The cost of
the war, and the loss of the territory, bankrupted the
Netherlands.

To recoup their fortunes, the Dutch turned Java into a
tropical estate, producing crops for sale in the European
market, of course to their considerable advantage. They
achieved this by applying the old Company's methods: an extra
tax, in the form of labour, was imposed on the Javanese.
Thus produce was extracted without paying the cultivators.
The Dutch had no money, and in any case no interest in
encouraging the import of manufactured goods which they did
not produce. The *Cultuurstelsel*, or Forced Cultivation
System, was in effect from 1830 to 1869. From the Dutch point
of view, it was a roaring success. Between 1831 and 1877
funds from the Indies, as the Dutch called their colony, paid
the debts of the Netherlands, the expenses of the war with
Belgium, as well as the cost of railways and public works. On
average, the Indies contributed nearly half the Dutch annual
budget. This is probably as pure and unarguable a case of
state exploitation as may be found anywhere; there was no
pretence that the labour tax imposed on the peasants was to
pay for services rendered. Indeed, these were reduced rather
than increased; education and welfare needs were ignored.
Not surprisingly, the word 'colonialism' to Indonesians,
particularly the Javanese, is a synonym for unscrupulous
rapacity. There is little doubt that social and economic
progress was arrested; Java would be far more developed if
some of the profits of the system had been invested in the
country at the time. Perhaps the only benefit it gained was

the introduction of new plants; tea, tobacco, cinnamon, palm-oil, and cinchona (for quinine). However, one must remember that it is wrong to impose present-day ethics on the past; the Dutch were only working on the assumption commonly held by all states at the time: namely that colonies are for the benefit of the possessing power.

The repeal of the Forced Cultivation System was not the result of any sudden attack of conscience, but simply due to the fact that its great profits had given rise to a Dutch middle class who now demanded, and obtained, the right to make money themselves in the Indies, thus inaugurating the 'Liberal' period of colonial administration. This coincided with the world boom towards the end of the century, and the Indies experienced a period of great prosperity. Simultaneously, the government turned its attention to the islands around Java, which it had previously neglected and, partly to prevent British encroachment, placed the boundaries of their colony where Indonesia's lie today, with the exception of Portuguese Timor, now incorporated. As part of this process of expansion, in 1873 they invaded Aceh, the last independent state in the archipelago. They met with fierce resistance. It was 1908 before the people were finally subdued; their 35-year struggle, against troops far better equipped, remains enshrined in Indonesian nationalist history as an example of heroic resistance.

The turn of the century saw the adoption of a more enlightened attitude, known as the 'Ethical Policy'. The Dutch, as some way of restituting, at least in part, the enormous amounts they had taken out of the country during the Forced Cultivation period, openly recognised a moral duty to the people of the Indies. Large sums were spent on welfare, derived from a boom period for tropical produce at the beginning of the century. Unfortunately, the Javanese were no better off, as their numbers continued to grow faster than the productivity of agriculture. From 2.5 million in 1800 the population had risen to 28 million in 1900. Increases in the amount of arable land, achieved through vast and expensive irrigation works, could not keep up with the growth in numbers, while migration to the less populous islands, even with government encouragement, made very little difference. As Dr. Demaine's article below shows, this problem of the balance between population and resources remains a constant preoccupation of Indonesia's government today.

The 'Ethical Policy' marked a significant change in another respect: the much wider provision of Western-type schooling to Indonesians. Until then, Dutch policy had been concerned to maintain the local cultures unchanged so far as possible. The new steps taken were hardly precipitate: in 1903 there we were 190,000 pupils throughout the Indies; by 1923 there were 700,000, and by 1940 2 million. These were not significant proportions of the relevant age-groups. Furthermore, the education provided was limited to primary and secondary; for higher education an Indonesian had to move to the alien environment of a Dutch school and so prepare himself for a university in the Netherlands. It is important to note, too, that most of the education was provided in Java, as being the most developed as well as the most populous of the islands.

Though the western-educated were few, there were even fewer opportunities for employment for them, and these were nearly all in government. This could not expand as rapidly as the schools were turning out their graduates. In this circum-stance one may trace the beginnings of nationalism and, event-ually, the eviction of the Dutch from the Indies. The first nationalist is, interestingly, a noblewoman, Kartini, daughter of a governor or *Regent*, one of the class who underpinned the Dutch position. Her diagnosis of her countrymen's discontents is of considerable importance for the understan-ding of present-day Indonesian attitudes. She argued that the Dutch, having introduced Indonesians to Western civilisa-tion, now attempted to limit their access ot it. She did not thank them for attempting to preserve Javanese culture, nor does she complain of any injury it might have suffered. In brief, the Dutch fault was that they were not Westernising Indonesia enough.

From this beginning, the nationalist movement developed fairly rapidly. The first significant nationalist party was the *Sarekat Islam*, founded in 1912. An extreme faction broke off in 1919 to form the *Partai Komunis di India*, or Communist Party of the Indies. It organised a revolt in 1926, which the government had little difficulty in putting down. The *PKI* was suppressed, and in 1927 the *Partai Nasional Indonesia (PNI)* was founded with as chairman an engineer called Sukarno, later to be independent Indonesia's first president. It inherited many former members of the *PKI*, and demanded complete political and economic independence for Indonesia, with an elected government, advocating non-co-operation with the Dutch as the means to its objective. Only two years later, Sukarno and other leaders of the organisation were arrested. Though he was released in 1931, his demagogy ensured his further arrest in 1933. Of considerable importance is the fact that the *Volksraad* or People's Council, carefully selected though it was, passed a resolution in 1936 proposing self-g vernment. The Dutch government rejected it two years later. Even those Indonesians who had been favourably disposed towards the Dutch now understood that if they wished to control their affairs it could be only on a basis of complete independence.

The outbreak of the Second World War gave the nationalists' cause powerful assistance. First, the Germans occupied Holland, so cutting it off from Indonesia. Then the Japanese invaded the Indies, meeting little resistance. In very short order all Europeans were interned, and Indonesian officials found themselves promoted to senior positions in the administration. The Japanese encouraged Indonesian nationalism, promised self-government soon, and organised and trained a home guard, called the *Peta*, officered by Indonesians (very few had been commissioned by the Dutch into their Colonial Army). They also released Sukarno and gave him the presidency of a Central Advisory Council they would consult on questions of administration. All this was done with an eye to obtaining support for the Japanese war effort, of course; nevertheless these measures established the nucleus of the future Indonesi esian state.

With the end of the war in the Pacific, Sukarno and Hatta, a prominent nationalist leader of Menangkabau origin, jointly declared independence on 17th August 1945; they were soon appointed President and Vice-President respectively. Recognition was denied the new Republic for over four years. In that period it had to fend off first the British, who were in the island primarily to take over from the Japanese, and then two armed attacks by the Dutch when they relieved the British. In addition, the infant state had to withstand two left-wing attempts to capture the Republic. Its struggle was crowned with success, however, only when, as a result of its skilful diplomacy, the United States decided to back Indonesian independence. Sovereignty was formally transferred at the end of 1949 to a federal state composed of the Javanese-led Republic and various states in the outer islands put together by the Dutch in an attempt to nullify its power. This Dutch-inspired federal structure was dismantled within a year, giving place to the present unitary state. The unfortunate consequence has been to throw suspicion on all subsequent attampts at federal solutions to the country's problems. It was also in this period that the basic principle of Indonesian foreign policy, that is to say 'independent and active', was established, as argued by Dr. Leifer later in this symposium. As he also shows, the experiences

of this period had a formative influence on the political
and military leaders' attitudes to the outside world.

The years from 1950 to the present may conveniently be
divided into three periods, distinguished by the form of
government. Until 1958 a form of parliamentary government
was followed; from 1959 to 1965 'Guided Democracy' held sway;
since 1966 a military regime, styling itself the 'New Order,
has been in power.

As is frequently the case after a revolution, the early
years of Indonesia's independence were marked by internal
conflicts; they involved ethnic, religious, and economic
factors. An attempt to achieve some resolution through the
adoption of parliamentary democracy came to nothing. By 1959,
when a system of 'Guided Democracy' was adopted, the new
dispensation was sufficiently clear. Indonesia was to be a
secular state. Islamic law was not to apply, for all that
95 per cent of Indonesians profess themselves Muslim, and
not even to them alone. Government was to be centralised;
there was no question of any federalism, nor of any considerable delegation of powers from the capital. It was also to
be authoritarian; 'representatives' were to be chosen from
above, not below. In foreign policy, the principle that
Indonesia was not to be tied to the policies of any other
country was forcibly reiterated. Most important, the
ultimate decisions were to be in the hands of members of
the Javanese ethnic group, or those who identified with them.

The next phase, from 1959 to 1966, decided whether the
country was to align itself in world affairs with the
Communist bloc, as it then was, with an internal political
system to match. 'Guided Democracy' was a means used by
President Sukarno to ensure suppression of any dissentient
voices again his and, generally, Javanese leadership. It
included as the major item a campaign to induce the Netherlands to hand over Western New Guinea. This involved on the
one hand greatly increasing the size and powers of the
Army; on the other, both to balance the military and to obtain
external Communist support for his campaign, Sukarno encouraged the growth of the Communist Party, the *PKI*. He acquired
the territory in 1962, and then immediately turned to oppose
the plan to create the Federation of Malaysia from Malaya,
Singapore, and the British Borneo territories. The *PKI* waxed
further in strength and began an agitation in the rural areas
of Java. Abroad, Sukarno drew closer to China and North
Korea. All this came to an abrupt climax in October 1965,
when some of his supporters in the *PKI* and the armed forces

engaged in an armed conspiracy which succeeded only in the murder of a number of leading generals. The counter-attack, mounted by General (as he then was) Suharto, effectively deposed Sukarno in his favour in 1966. This turn of events gave free rein to many, particularly Muslim zealots, who had been intimidated by one or other *PKI* organisation, to take their revenge. Estimates of the numbers who perished in the resulting massacres vary greatly, but a figure of 200,000 may not be too far off the mark.

The 'New Order', as the military regime styled itself, found it was governing a country ruined by the heavy military expenditure of Sukarno's foreign adventures and the general maladministration which had characterised 'Guided Democracy'. Seeing the cause of their country's misfortunes in the constant political turmoil since it declared its independence, the regime made it a cardinal point of policy, pursued over the succeeding years, that the country's energies were to be entirely devoted to development. In consequence, political opposition was not to be permitted. So that while, for reasons unclear, the form of parliamentary democracy was to be followed, its content was to be voided. The activities of opposition political parties were to be severely restricted, while they themselves were to be emasculated. On the other hand, a government-supporting party was to be created and heavily backed. With regard to foreign affairs, the constant pre-occupation with them evinced by the previous regime was to be eschewed. Relations with the Communist states were to be avoided as far as possible. Aid was essential; it was to be sought whence it was most available, that is the Western democracies, but this cupboard love involved no ideological commitment. When it came to the practice of government, the division of labour was roughly as follows. The military concerned themselves with ensuring political stability, that is to say the suppression of all expressions of opposition, and with external security. Development policies, subject to their overall supervision, they entrusted to civilian officials.

The extent to which the 'New Order' has produced the prosperity which it seeks as its legitimation is discussed below by Dr. Harvey Demaine and Mr. John Walton. I myself give an account of how the process of integrating the country is proceeding, while Dr. Angela Hobart discusses the role of the performing arts in the present day. Finally Dr. Michael Leifer, considers the extent to which the regime's foreign policy has remained 'independent and active'.

2 Population and resources

HARVEY DEMAINE

Throughout the modern history of the territories which today comprise the Republic of Indonesia, there have been widely contrasting views of the country's resource endowment in relation to its population. On the one hand Indonesia has been seen as a veritable eldorado, with a natural resource base capable of supporting a population several times the present number at a standard of living at least on a par with the developed world. On the other hand, Indonesia's large population (estimated at about 160 million by 1984) is seen as a millstone preventing any significant improvement of living standards and threatening to drag the country into the abyss in both economic and political terms, such as occurred in the slaughter which followed the attempted coup by members of the Communist Party of Indonesia (PKI) in 1965.(2)

The subsequent recovery of Indonesia has once again stimulated the first of the two contrasting views above, in the view that the country could become the regional economic superpower of Southeast Asia. Since 1967, Indonesia's economy has grown at an extremely rapid rate, averaging over 7 per cent growth in gross domestic product per annum throughout the 1970s, and 9.6 per cent in 1979-80, second in the world only to the nearby island republic of Singapore. This growth has taken place within the context of a major volte-face in national policy, expressed above all in the new emphasis given to attracting foreign investment and in the careful economic

management strategies of a group of technocrats educated at
the University of California at Berkeley and led by Professors
Widjojo Nitisastro and Ali Wardhana.(3) In particular, the
new investment climate stimulated exploration, discovery and
production of major new resources of hydrocarbons which turned
Indonesia into one of the world's major oil producers outside
the Middle East.

The economic performance of Indonesia over the past decade
and a half has seemed to suggest that the country is finally
beginning to achieve its potential and to take the place in
the world long expected of it. As Charles Fisher (1967, p.122)
has pointed out, such a belief began with the initial penetration of the area in the Age of Discovery when the spices of
the Moluccas attracted traders first from Portugal and subsequently from the Low Countries. As far as the Dutch who
began the formal colonisation of the territories of Indonesia
were concerned, this view of the great wealth of the archipelago continued throughout their rule and the territory came
to be regarded as 'the cork by which Holland floated'. By
1939 the development of the tropical export economy of the
archipelago had progressed to an extent that one writer has
stated that Indonesia 'was the greatest producer of raw
materials in the world'.(Luthy 1965, p.84)

This too was a belief held by the leaders of the Republic of
Indonesia in the heady period which followed the seizure of
independence from the Dutch in 1945, which the latter eventually accepted in the course of negotiations in 1949-50.
Official statements of the new government claimed that
Indonesia was 'the third richest country in the world in
natural resources, after the United States and the Soviet
Union' (Report on Indonesia 8(1), 1965, p.15) and the
country's charismatic President Sukarno seems also to have been
firmly convinced of the fact, assuming that any troubles which
faced the nation could be attributed to the continuing neo-
colonial framework in which the country operated. Greater
insulation from the world economy was held to be the means by
which the Indonesian people could utilise the country's
natural resources for the improvement of their own living
standards, particularly if the Republic were to secure control
of Irian Jaya (then West New Guinea) which the Dutch had
retained after 1950 and which in itself was proof that the
territory was indeed an eldorado 'floating upon a sea of oil'.
(Fisher 1967, p.168)

Fisher 1967, 1972) has successfully exploded some of the

more fanciful assumptions concerning the Indonesian resource base. As he points out, the idea that the luxuriance of the tropical forest vegetation cover, which is the climax in most of the Indonesian archipelago, is an indication of great soil fertility can now be dismissed and replaced by a view stressing the fragility of most tropical soils once the vegetation cover has been removed. Similarly he demonstrates that, far from being the world's greatest raw material producer in the pre World War II period, Indonesia's total raw material output was, in value terms, substantially less even than British production of coal and less in per capita terms than the output of its near neighbour, Peninsular Malaysia (Fisher 1967, pp.197-4). Moreover the experience of the Sukarno era in Indonesia (1950-65), under a president who might well have been guilty of misquoting Henry Ford to the effect that 'economics is bunk', amply demonstrates that whatever wealth Indonesia possesses is no guarantee of a prosperous future for the country's people without adequate management.

Indeed, by the end of the Sukarno era it would have been difficult to contradict the other view of Indonesia suggested above, for the Republic was amongst the poorest countries of the world with a stagnant, deflationary economic situation, a rate of inflation of over 200 per cent, with minimal foreign exchange reserves and little in the way of foreign investment. In the absence of investment in the rehabilitation of infrastructure and production facilities, output in several of the country's major economic sectors was actually declining and in the countryside of Java in particular evidence of real poverty and deprivation was growing. It was upon the basis of such hardships that the PKI began to attract support and on which it believed it had sufficient backing to attempt the coup of 1965. Only the prompt action of the present President, then General, Suharto with other more junior army leaders thwarted the planned takeover, although the impression that rural Java is a powder-keg just waiting to explode still has currency among commentators at the present time (May 1978).(4) Indeed the concern of the West for the future stability of the country very much explains the willingness of the Western powers to establish the so-called Inter-Governmental Group for Indonesia (IGGI) to bail out the Republic in financial terms after 1965. (5) It is clear that such a strategy has succeeded in the short term at least, but the philosophy behind it seems to be in direct contradiction to the idea of Indonesia as an economic superpower about to achieve take-off.

It is with an assessment of these basically inconsistent views of Indonesia that the remainder of this chapter is

concerned, for such an assessment is basic to any discussion
of the future development of the economy and society of the
country; to, as it were, an 'understanding of Indonesia'. The
chapter will proceed by examining the dimensions of the
country's population problem, with special reference to the
metropolitan island of Java. Thereafter attention will be
paid to the possibilities of relieving this problem, particularly in relation to the wider exploitation of the land
resources of the Outer Islands.(6) Finally attention will be
turned to the wider aspects of Indonesia's resource base in
the context of the scope for industrialisation as a means of
shifting the balance of population and resources in the country
and of offering an improved standard of living to a wider
spectrum of the population.

THE POPULATION QUESTION

It is not difficult to see why the more pessimistic view of
Indonesia's future prospects has quite common currency at the
present time, despite the recent high levels of economic
growth. At the 1980 census Indonesia recorded a total population of 147.49 million, growing at the rate of 2.34 per cent
per annum over the intercensal period 1971-80. Even this
large figure, which made Indonesia the world's fifth largest
state in demographic terms after China, India, the Soviet
Union and the United States, was generally considered to be an
underestimate by some 3 per cent (Hull 1981, p.115) and
observers suggest that the 1980 population was in fact at least
150 million, giving a level of 160 million by 1984. Perhaps
more disturbing than the actual total, however, was the still
high rate of population growth which surprised many Indonesians who had begun to believe that the country's family
planning programme was beginning to have a considerable
impact. In fact it is suggested that the rate of natural
increase at the end of the intercensal period (1979-80) had in
fact declined to about 1.9-2.0 per cent per annum, but the
continuation of even this trend is now estimated to result in
a population of 222 million by the year 2000. (Glassburner
and Poffenberger 1983, p.23) And even this figure will not
be the stopping point, but merely a brief transitional level
on the way to an ultimate stationary population of around
325 million which might be reached by the year 2060. (Hull and
Mantra 1981, p.283)

Such a population total is disturbing when one considers
the conditions which exist in parts of Indonesia even today.
On the island of Java, Indonesia can boast some of the highest

rural population densities in the world. Of the total population of 147 million recorded in the census of 1980, over 91 million were concentrated on this single island, giving it an overall population density of 629 persons per square kilometre, but with particular areas far in excess of this level. Table 2.1 illustrates the population densities in 1980 for the various provinces of Java and the adjacent island of Bali which shares some of its characteristics, but certain regencies (counties) already had even higher densities in 1971, with Bantul in Jogyakarta Special District recording 1,122 persons per square kilometre and Klaten, near Surakarta in Central Java, reaching as much as 1,570 per square kilometre.

Table 2.1
Java and Bali: Population Densities 1980

Province	Population 1980 (mn)	Area (km^2)	Density (per km^2)
West Java	27.49	44,599	616
Jakarta	6.51	593	10,980
Central Java	25.37	37,100	684
Jogyakarta	2.75	3,186	863
East Java	29.18	47,922	609
Bali	2.47	5,591	442

Source: Hull 1981, p.117.

Densities of this order in mainly rural areas imply extremely small agricultural land holdings and, as Table 2.2 shows, taking figures from the Agricultural Census of 1973, these average no more than 0.6 hectares per household. Many, however, are even smaller.

Table 2.2
Java and Bali
Smallholder Agriculture: Average Size of Holdings 1973

Province	No. Holdings	Area of Holdings (ha)	Ave. Holding (ha)
West Java	2,468,281	1,524,965	0.62
Central Java	2,765,861	1,753,304	0.63
Jogyakarta	343,572	181,375	0.53
East Java	3,066,218	2,026,336	0.66
Bali	305,154	266,605	0.87

Source: Indonesia, Central Bureau of Statistics 1976.

Table 2.3 demonstrates that at least one-third of all agricultural holdings in Java in 1973 were less than half of the
provincial average, with the figure rising to 42 per cent in
the case of West Java province and 47 per cent in Yogyakarta
Special District. The modal value varies between 0.2–0.3
hectares per farm in East Java and Bali to a mere 0.1–0.2
hectares in the other provinces..Table 2.3 also shows the
average area of agricultural land (cropland) per capita in
each province which, as can be seen, works out at no more than
one-eleventh to one-sixteenth of one hectare per person.
These latter figures are based upon the 1971 population of
Java of 76.1 million; as has already been noted this total had
risen by 1980 to 91.3 million, further reducing the average
area of agricultural land per capita to a little over 0.05
hectares.

Table 2.3
Java and Bali
Distribution of Holdings by Size of Holding 1973
(Cropland Only) (%)

Holding Size (ha)	West Java	C. Java	Jogya	E. Java	Bali
Less than 0.1	6.06	2.38	4.37	1.92	0.59
0.1 - 0.2	19.30	16.90	23.38	16.49	9.23
0.2 - 0.3	17.00	16.57	19.17	16.69	13.44
0.3 - 0.4	11.44	13.55	11.94	12.42	11.98
0.4 - 0.5	8.29	9.88	8.17	8.33	9.26
0.5 - 0.6	7.79	8.86	7.47	9.49	11.14
0.6 - 0.75	6.89	8.52	5.94	8.20	9.02
0.75 - 1.0	7.06	8.49	6.49	9.39	9.54
1.0 - 2.0	11.87	11.46	10.39	12.96	16.90
over 2.0	4.30	3.38	2.18	4.11	8.90

Average Area of Cropland per Capita (ha)

	West Java	C. Java	Jogya	E. Java	Bali
	0.070	0.061	0.063	0.060	0.091

Source: Indonesia, Central Bureau of Statistics 1976.

These aggregate figures bear ample testimony to the pressure
of population on land resources which exists today in Java
and, to a slightly lesser extent, Bali. Although the quality
of land and its productivity must, of course, be taken into
account, the details of average holding size and land area per
capita serve to point a stark picture of rural overcrowding
in which it would be difficult to imagine the bulk of holdings

17

offering a reasonable standard of living even with the highest
yields currently being achieved in Southeast Asia for paddy
rice.   Even those holdings larger than the average may not off
offer much more favourable possibilities.   Moreover a comparison of the number of agricultural holdings in each province of Java with the total population of the respective
provinces is instructive here.   If one calculates that each
holding is worked by a family of five persons on average, then
it is clear that there are still substantial numbers of the
population without access to agricultural land.   A rough cal-
culation, presented in Table 2.4, puts this figure at just
under 30 million people, or 41 per cent of Java's rural/non-
metropolitan population.

Table 2.4
Java: Estimates of Landlessness 1971-73

Province Province	No. Agri. Holdings (a)	Popn. with Access to Land (a)x5=(b)(mn)	Total Population (c)(mn)	Rural Landless % (c-b/c x 100)
West Java	2,468,281	12.34	21.63	42.9
Cent. Java	2,765,861	13.83	23.50	41.2
Jogyakarta	343,572	1.72	2.51	31.5
East Java	3,066,218	15.33	25.53	40.0
		43.22	73.17	40.9
Add Urban Population		6.05		
		49.27		32.7

Of course Java, as Indonesia's metropolitan island, has a
sizeable urban population, but in 1971 this numbered only
10.6 million in total including Jakarta, the capital city,
with its population of 4.55 million.   Thus the urban population for the remainder of Java totalled only 6.05 million,
a figure which added to the rural population with access to
land still leaves some 23.9 million persons (32.7 per cent)
unaccounted for.   It is recognised that the rural population
is not synonymous with the agricultural population, but these
approximate figures again serve to suggest a further dimension
of Java's population problem, namely the large numbers of
landless families in the rural areas.

This situation of rural landlessness, the existence of which
is supported by detailed village studies undertaken by the
Agro-Economic Survey of Indonesia (Sajogyo 1972, p.3; Collier
et al. 1982) and by the International Rice Research Institute

(Ihalauw and Utami 1975; Prabowo and Sajogyo 1975), has traditionally been supported by communal distribution mechanisms
within Javanese villages. Those with land have been obliged by
by social custom and sanction to offer a living to the landless through the use of their labour in harvesting the staple
rice crop, payment being made in the form of a share of the
individual harvester's crop. This system, known as 'bawon' in
some parts of Java, and the use of poor families also for
milling rice by traditional methods have led to a situation in
the Javanese countryside which the anthropologist Clifford
Geertz (1963) has described as 'agricultural involution', a
process of 'sharing poverty' whereby more and more people gain
their living from a limited area of agricultural land in order
to maintain the stability of the village community. However,
in modern times there is ample evidence that such mechanisms
have been breaking down, that the communal harvesting system
has been extended to a degree that even the landowners have
been unable to make an adequate living. They have begun to
react against this and in certain areas have changed to the
use of wage labour gangs controlled by local merchants as a
less wasteful methods of harvesting (Collier, Wiradi and
Soentoro 1973; Collier, Soentoro, Wiradi and Makali 1974;
Hayami and Hafid 1979; Collier 1978). (7) This, the wider use
of mechanised rice milling (Timmer 1972, 1973; Sadli 1973;
Collier, Colter, Sinarhadi and Shaw 1974; Timmer 1974) and the
more recent adoption in some areas of small two-wheel
tractors (Sinaga 1978, 1981a, 1981b; Collier *et al.* 1982;
Lingard and Wicks 1983, p.99; Lingard and Bagyo 1983) have had
the effect of forcing many landless families out of even
these marginal occupations in the rural areas.

Such events, which have been in turn associated with the
introduction of the seed-fertiliser technology of the 'Green
Revolution' in Javanese agriculture via the 'Bimas' programme
(Mears 1970; Birowo 1975), have precipitated a further manifestation of the population problem on that island, the rapid
growth of the urban centres as people have moved out of the
countryside in search of a better or more assured living. It
has been estimated that between 1961 and 1971 almost 1.1
million people migrated to the urban areas of Indonesia, which
increased by over 10 per cent by this mechanism alone (Collier
et al. 1982).. Most of this movement was channelled to the
single focus of Jakarta which alone gained over 900,000 net
migrants who contributed over 54 per cent of the net population
growth from 2.91 million in 1961 to 4.55 million in 1971
(Hugo 1979, p.192). By 1984 the capital's population had
risen even more dramatically to almost 7 million (Specter
1984, p.23).

The rapid movement of population into urban areas, particularly Jakarta, allied to a high rate of natural increase among the mainly youthful urban population, not surprisingly has created major social problems in the cities. (8) To the casual casual visitor for whom Jakarta *is* Indonesia the population problem is immediately visible in the growth of the great squatter areas of that city, many of which lie in stark juxtaposition to the modern business and commercial sectors of the capital. As early as 1961 one estimate of the number of squatters in Jakarta was as high as 750,000 (Hanna 1961, p.4) which has been extrapolated to give a squatter population of 1.14 million in 1971. A World Bank estimate, however, suggested that as many as 3.8 million people were living in what they termed 'minimum standard areas' by 1975 (Laquian 1979, p.53), areas deemed to be lacking in adequate housing and public utilities. With the city estimated to have a housing stock adequate for only half a million people, but supporting ten times as many, it is scarcely surprising that population densities as high as 100,000 persons per square kilometre have been recorded in the Glodok-Tambora area in the old core of the city, where domestic water supplies have to be purchased from vendors, there being no piped supplies or even local wells (Krausse 1978, 15ff). Marginal living conditions such as these indicate a similarly marginal economic situation, with most families resident in such areas typically making their living from the tertiary sector in which individual occupations may be sub-divided among friends and relatives, enabling each to keep body and soul together. Indeed the conditions in these occupations in the city mirror to a great extent those in the countryside, leading McGee (1973) to term such people 'peasants in the city' and to borrow the term 'urban involution' for the idea of shared poverty in the city from Geertz's use in the countryside already mentioned.

Given the situation in the rural and urban areas of Java described above, the question arises as to just how bad the living conditions of sections of the Indonesian population have become, to what extent they are enjoying less than the minimum acceptable standards of nutrition, housing, medical care, education and other social amenities. In answer to this, it is possible to turn to recent estimates of absolute poverty levels in Indonesia based upon real standards of nutritional intake, most of which derive from surveys carried out since 1963-64 by the Central Bureau of Statistics and generally known as the SUSENAS (household consumption) surveys. A study under the auspices of FAO took 1969-70 SUSENAS data to estimate calorie and protein intake of expenditure groups.

The results of this survey indicated that for fully 57 per cent of households in rural Java the average daily *per capita* energy and protein intake was 1,400 calories and 34 grammes of protein, well below any medically accepted minimum (Booth and Sundrum 1981, p.206). (9) Averages in the rest of Indonesia were higher than in rural Java, but even so an estimated 28 per cent of households in rural areas in Outer Indonesia consumed an average of 1,560 calories and 37 grammes of protein *per capita*. The FAO survey also made the point that urban families at similar or even higher expenditure levels consumed even less energy and protein than rural households given the higher cost of food and greater proportion of cash expenditures in the urban areas. A second commentator, van Ginneken (1976) concurred with these interpretations and concluded that 'over four-fifths of the urban population and three-fifths of the rural population were living in poverty in terms of both calorie and protein intake', while Sajogyo (1975) has suggested, on the basis of a poverty line of 360 kgs. of rice equivalent consumed per month in urban areas and 240 kgs. in rural areas, that 57 per cent of the rural population and 54 per cent of the urban population in Java fell below this line and therefore suffered from absolute poverty.

Although there has been criticism of these conclusions, it seems permissible from the available evidence to conclude that a not-insignificant proportion of households in both rural and urban Java had dietary standards unacceptably low by most medical criteria at the beginning of the 1970s. Nor had the situation changed much for the better by 1976. A further SUSENAS survey at that date has been interpreted as showing a fall in *per capita* calorie consumption among the poorest 40 per cent of the population everywhere in Indonesia except for the urban areas of Java. In rural areas of Java in particular, it is likely that average calorie intake fell a few percentage points (Dapice 1981, p.79). There is some question whether the deterioration was a voluntary shift away from cheaper foods such as cassava and corn into the preferred, but less calorie-intensive, rice staple but, on the other hand, these other cereal crops did increase in price between 1970 and 1976 which may have been the major factor in the decline in calorific intake and a sign of a relatively worsening situation among the poorer sectors of the population.

SOLUTIONS TO THE POPULATION PROBLEM?

The overall picture of the situation in Java is thus one which
scarcely gives rise to optimism and appears to confirm the
rather gloomy assessment of the prospects for Indonesia outlined earlier. The time has come, however, to make two
important qualifications to the argument rendered thus far.
The first of these is that the discussion of population
pressure has been focused entirely on the situation on the
metropolitan island of Java with neighbouring Madura and Bali.
These islands, despite their dominant position in demographic
terms, constitute no more than one-thirteenth to one-fourteenth
of the total land area of the Republic. The other 93 per cent
of Indonesia's territory, over 1.88 million square milometres,
contained in 1980 a population of only 56 million persons at
an average density of only 30 persons per square kilometre
(Table 2.5)

Table 2.5
Outer Indonesia: Population Densities 1980

Island	Population(mn)	Area(km^2)	Density(per km^2)
Sumatra	28.016	485,805	57.7
Kalimantan	6.723	553,000	12.2
Sulawesi	10.410	202,693	51.4
Irian Jaya	1.174	410,660	2.9
Others	9.897	152,960	64.7
	56.220	1805,118	31.1

Source: Hull 1981, p.117

These figures immediately suggest that Indonesia's population
problem may not be purely a matter of over-population, but
rather a problem of maldistribution of that population in
relation to the available resources, so that the problem
might be alleviated at least in part by the transfer of population to develop the extensive lands available in the Outer
Islands. The second qualification is that the situation in
Java itself is not static, but rather one which must be
reviewed in the light of improvements in technology which
themselves require the reassessment of resources. In particular it must be pointed out that Javanese agriculture has
developed rapidly over the past decade and that Indonesia may
also have considerable industrial resource potential which may
make the population concentration in Java an ideal base for
industrialisation. In such circumstances the concentration of
the bulk of Indonesia's population in Java might be viewed as
no different essentially from similar concentrations in the
Northeast part of the United States or in the Rhine axis in

Western Europe.

In turning to the other side of the equation of population and resources in Indonesia, we consider first the fundamental question of whether the country will be able in the future to feed itself from its own land resources or at least attain a higher level of self-sufficiency than is the case at the present time. Of this ex-President Sukarno had no doubt, being convinced that the main population problem was indeed maldistribution. As late as 1964 the President is said to have declared 'My solution is to exploit more land - because if you exploit all the land in Indonesia you can feed 250 million ' (quoted in Hull and Mantra 1981, p.264). As has been demonstrated, this indeed may be necessary in the not too distant future and it is important for Indonesia if vital foreign exchange is not to be eaten up by food imports that the bulk of the food supplies should be produced internally.

TRENDS IN FOOD PRODUCTION

In assessing the possibilities in this direction, two points are clear. First there is still scope for improvement of yields on the area already planted in Indonesia. Indeed substantial improvements have already been made over the last decade, particularly in the rice sector in Java. From a total paddy rice production of just over 23 million tonnes in 1976, production has been pushed up to almost 43 million tonnes in 1981, giving a total production of *milled* rice of 23 million tonnes. This has been the result of the extensive investment in the rehabilitation and improvement of the irrigation systems of Java since 1967 as well as the steady expansion of the technology of intensification mentioned above. With the introduction after 1978 of a further round of new high-yielding varieties resistant to the *wereng* or brown planthopper, yields have continued their upward climb to reach close on four tonnes per hectare and farmers have been able to add a second or third rice crop into their cropping systems (Collier *et al.* 1982, 11ff). (10) Thus by 1981 the government was reported to have accumulated a stockpile of some two million tonnes of rice for emergency use and food imports in 1982 had dropped to slightly less than 400,000 tonnes (McCawley 1983, p.22).

The crucial question is whether this dramatic upturn in food production can be sustained into the 1980s. Evidence from the last two years (1982-83) suggests unfortunately that the upward trend in production may have levelled off. Output in 1982 now appears to have been no higher than in 1981, while estimates for 1983 indicate a decline to little more than 20 million tonnes of milled rice (McCawley 1983, p.21), with the re-emergence of a new biotype of the *wereng*, drought and increasing defaults on rural credit payments variously responsible (Glassburner and Poffenberger 1983, p.21). Moreover, the basic rehabilitation of the irrigation systems of Java is now well nigh complete, so that future production increases will have to come from expensive investment in increasing cropping intensities in existing systems (World Bank 1978, p.18; Collier *et al*. 1982, p.10). This may be a more difficult proposition.

On the other hand, it is clear that there is scope for further increase in food production from the Outer Islands of Indonesia, whether rice or in the production of other staple foods such as cassava and corn. Thus far these latter crops have tended to be neglected in the government's concentration upon rice and when the framework of an all-cereals food production policy was examined for Repelita III (11), it was found that the basic research effort for an effective intensification programme for these crops was still largely absent (Mears and Moeljono 1981, p.40). As recent agro-ecological studies of parts of the Outer Islands have demonstrated, however, there is real potential even with the use of traditional techniques to step up yields (Metzner 1982). As far as rice is concerned, planted area in the Outer Islands is only a little less than that of Java at just over 4 million hectares, but yields are substantially lower at 2,733 kgs. per hectare in 1977 compared to Java's 3,550 kgs./ha. Further development of water control facilities in such islands as Sulawesi could effect an improvement in this direction, while there are hopes too of a major increase in cultivated area from the development of riceland in the tidal swamplands of Sumatra and Kalimantan. In Repelita II (1974-79), it was expected that almost one million hectares could be developed in such areas, at least partly in the form of large estates (Booth 1977, 56ff). Subsequently it appeared that further study was required of the water management problems of such schemes, and the target was substantially revised (Hanson 1981, p.222 3). At present the project is going ahead slowly mainly in the context of planned resettlement schemes under the transmigration programme, which attempts to shift population from Java to colonise the more empty lands of Outer Indonesia.

THE POPULATION REDISTRIBUTION PROGRAMME

Transmigration and its predecessor of the colonial period,
'colonisation', have been a feature of Indonesian policy
towards the population problem of Java since the first decade
of the present century. Indeed such a programme has been seen
as *the* answer to the metropolitan island's overcrowding and
was very much the context of President Sukarno's statement
quoted above. In fact it has proved more difficult to effect
a successful colonisation of the apparently extensive land
resources of the Outer Islands than was ever anticipated.
This difficulty relates to the marked differences in the
physical resource base which exist between Java (and Bali)
on the one hand and most of the rest of Indonesia on the
other. Not only does Java have a more seasonal climate than
the other major islands, several of which straddle the equator,
but its soils are naturally more fertile as a result of the
weathering of the neutral-basic rocks which characterise the
island's mountainous volcanic core. In the Outer Islands
there are major tracts which are non-volcanic, their base
material being mainly crystalline massifs which break down
into acid, rather infertile soils and, with a few exceptions
such as the *Cultuurgebiet*, the plantation zone of Northeast
Sumatra, the volcanic source material is also acidic. These
bedrock characteristics and the heavy all-year round rainfall
experienced in Sumatra, Kalimantan and parts of Sulawesi
mean that the soil, once exposed from the natural forest
vegetation, rapidly loses fertility and the intensive cultivation pattern of Java has proved difficult to maintain in the
Outer Islands. Indeed, the early colonists in southern
Sumatra frequently reverted to the shifting method of cultivation to make a living after unsuccessful attempts at rice
cultivation in such regions (Utomo 1967, p.293; Suratman and
Guinness 1977, p.94).

In fact, experience of the transmigration process in Outer
Indonesia suggests that agricultural development in such areas
may not be served best by the promotion of annual food-crop
production. Where this has been the traditional goal as in
the south Sumatran province of Lampung, the main focus of
migration until recently, it has served only to export the
Javanese problem to another area of Indonesia (Hardjono 1977,
20ff; Arndt 1983, p.56). Thus recently greater emphasis has
been placed within transmigration schemes upon an expansion of
commercial cropping, particularly of tree crops such as rubber
and oil palm which would serve to recreate the forest environment destroyed by colonisation (Suratman and Guinness 1977;

Hardjono 1978). This is important since, apart from the coastal swamplands, much of the land resource in the Outer Islands is composed of hilly, quite steeply sloping ground which would be extremely susceptible to erosion if not used with care.(12) However, development of such land for tree crops requiring some years to mature implies an extensive financial outlay on the part of the government, and the proportion of the development budget absorbed by the trans-migration effort has shown a marked expansion over the last decade from a mere 0.7 per cent of the total in 1969-70 to 6.1 per cent in 1982-83 (Arndt 1983, p.66). A significant proportion of the increased budget has in fact been provided by the World Bank, loans from which have enabled a dramatic expansion in the scope of the programme from 46,100 families moved during Repelita I (1969-74) to 88,000 families during Repelita II and 286,000 families in the first four years of Repelita III (1979-83). During the same period, however, costs per family have risen twenty-fold and the programme is no longer a low-cost option which would be vulnerable if funds available were subject to contraction.(13)

Despite the increased scope of the transmigration programme, therefore, it is now generally recognised that it is never likely to be an effective method of reducing the population problems of Java. Even if it were possible to sustain a programme at the target rate envisaged (but not achieved) under Repelita III of 100,000 families moved each year, this figure would remove only one-fifth of the annual increase in Java's population (Arndt 1983, p.51). The process may con-tribute to the expansion of economic activity in the Outer Islands,(14) widening the country's overall economic base for the future, but it will scarcely reduce the existing dis-parities in levels of living between such areas and impover-ished Java.(15) It seems clear that the solution to the problem of the latter must in the end be found in other directions, firstly through a major effort to stabilise the population of Java so that the situation does not worsen dramatically and secondly through an attempt to turn Java into the metropolitan core of Indonesia much more in the accepted sense of core-periphery models, that is through the intensified development of an industrial base centred upon ample supplies of cheap labour and the further exploitation of the country's natural resources.(16)

FAMILY PLANNING POLICIES

The first of these measures must be seen naturally as a long-term palliative since Indonesia has only relatively recently turned to family planning as a major component of national development. President Sukarno's pro-natalist position restricted efforts to the non-governmental sector until 1965 and it was only in 1969 that a true national policy was formulated with the foundation of the National Family Planning Coordinating Board. Since then again with the assistance of foreign aid organisations, the programme has expanded rapidly so that by 1977 some 58 per cent of women considered eligible in Java and Bali were claimed to have accepted some form of contraception.(Cho *et al.* 1980, p.77) Unfortunately, such claims must be treated with some caution. Commentators on the programme note that there is a degree of double-counting with previous users returning to contraception being treated as new acceptors, while surveys suggest that, during intensive pushes to reach planned targets many 'acceptors' do no more than that, without ever actually using the contraceptives. (Hull and Mantra 1981, p.270; Hull 1976, pp.108-9) Levels of *use* appear to be rather in the order of 30 per cent and in any case the preferred family size in Java remains at four children per family. (Hull 1976, p.110) There is no doubt that the rate of natural increase in Indonesia, especially in Java and Bali, is falling, not only from the increased use of family planning techniques, but also from the rather later date of marriage; however, given the educational and logistic problems involved, it would appear to be optimistic to expect a very rapid decline in fertility in the country over a short period. Perhaps the main hope is that the stabilisation of population can in the end be brought forward and set at a lower level than previously forecast.

PROSPECTS FOR INDUSTRIALISATION

Much more promising in the short term as a measure to alleviate the more pessimistic scenarios which might stem from the socio-economic situation in Java is the effort to transform the structure of that island's economy through a major push towards industrialisation. This has been, in fact, an important element in government policy ever since the advent of the New Order government of General Suharto in 1967, with the passing of the Foreign and Domestic Investment Laws, designed to encourage private enterprise to take a much greater role in the country's economic development. Foreign investment in particular has indeed been attracted, especially from Japan, being channelled mainly in two directions, on the one hand into the exploitation of raw materials for export and on the other into modern sector industries to replace consumer goods previously imported. Overall the impact of such investment must be reckoned to have been thus far a little disappointing. The manufacturing sector still accounts for no more than 12.7 per cent of Gross Domestic Product (GDP), while in a country in which cheap labour must be one of the comparative advantages, the role of the modern manufacturing sector in creating employment opportunities has been rather limited. Manufacturing as a whole only accounted for 8.6 per cent of total employment in 1977 and the bulk of this (over three-quarters) was to be found in rural areas, largely among household and small-scale industries. (Poot 1981, p.85)(17) Moreover, heavily protected as they are behind tariff barriers, many industries continue to be inefficient producers with little prospect of development into exporting industries. Meanwhile investments in resource development have produced exports mainly in raw material form with low value-added and limited effects on the wider industrial sector.

Since the mid-1970s, it has been realised that there are limitations on industrialisation in the import-substitution mould in Southeast Asia. Several countries in the region have begun to seek a new strategy attempting to establish a firmer industrial base on the comparative advantages of indigenous raw materials and cheap labour. Indonesia too has followed this course of action. Here the further question arises as to how adequate is the country's raw material base for the support of such industrial growth, a question which returns to the oft-held view of Indonesia as one of the world's major natural resource producers. It is to this question that we finally turn in the present chapter in an examination of the country's base in industrial raw materials.

Prior to the outbreak of the Second World War the reputation of Indonesia (or the Netherlands Indies as it then was) as a major raw material producer was founded mainly upon tropical agricultural produce. These contributed over 60 per cent of export earnings and the country was the world's largest exporter of copra, palm oil, pepper, quinine, kapok and tapioca, as well as being on the threshold of taking the lead in rubber. It was the second largest exporter of sisal and took third place in both tea and coffee. Shortly after the war these various commodities accounted for as much as 80 per cent of exports. Today the situation has changed dramatically.

By the mid-1970s a single commodity, petroleum, had become the dominant factor in the economy, contributing 72 per cent of exports by value and providing the bulk of government revenues from taxes and royalties. Although there has been some decline in the volume of oil exports in the past few years, price increases and the rise of natural gas production have served to maintain the dominance of hydrocarbons as the most important natural resource for Indonesia (Table 2.6).

Given this paramount position, any assessment of Indonesia's prospects on the basis of raw material production must begin with the hydrocarbons sector. It is in relation to its position as an oil-producer that the country is best known in the West at the present time. Indonesia's importance in this field is testified by the country's membership of the Organisation of Petroleum Exporting Countries (OPEC), among which it is much the most important producer and exporter in the Far East, where it is second only to China in terms of total production. Indonesia takes on a particular significance ficance as a major supplier of oil to Japan, now one of the world's largest and most rapidly growing economies, which in 1979 purchased 57 per cent of Indonesia crude and condensates. (Ooi 1982, p.17) At the same time, however, it is important to keep this position in perspective. Supplies from Indonesia make up no more than 12-15 per cent of Japanese oil imports (18) and until the recent OPEC production cutbacks Indonesia was ranked only in the order of twelfth to fourteenth among the world's producers with an annual output of about 1.6 million barrels per day (580 million barrels per year) which may be compared with Britain's current production of over 2 million barrels per day.(19) This level of production amounted to only 2.5 per cent of the world's supplies and estimates of reserves put these at a similar proportion of the world total.

Nevertheless our assessment of Indonesia's position as a producer of hydrocarbons should be focused on the significance of petroleum for the country itself and this cannot be over-stressed, particularly in relation to the way that petroleum has helped transform the economy since 1965. Indonesia as the Netherlands Indies was, of course, a significant producer of oil in the colonial period and was the original home of the Royal Dutch Shell group, but like so many other aspects of the economy the petroleum sector began to run down in the Sukarno era and it was only with the change in investment climate created by the passing of the Foreign Investment Law in 1967 that attention began to turn once again to the archipelago as a major supplier of oil. This and related legislation

provided very favourable contractual relationships for the oil
companies and with the improvement of offshore exploration and
drilling technology attention was attracted to Southeast Asia
as a whole to balance the excessive concentration of the
West's supplies in a politically unstable Middle East. Since
1967 the coastal and internal waters of Indonesia in particular have become a veritable patchwork of oil company concessions, many of which have been rapidly rewarded by discoveries of commercial quantities of petroleum.(20)

The key to the rise of Indonesia as an oil producer lies in
the underlying geology of the archipelago. Geophysical
surveys have revealed that the continental shelves of the area
are occupied by up to forty basins created in the Tertiary
geological period, many of which contain the trap structures
necessary for the accumulation of commercial hydrocarbons
resources. Indeed since the expansion of offshore exploration,
drilling has achieved encouragingly high success rates, at
least on a par with the Middle East.(21) Discoveries have
served to place Indonesia's reserves at an official 10.2
billion barrels of oil, but as can be seen from Figure 2.1
several important basins have yet to be fully explored and
several commentators have recently made claims for a substantial upgrading of reserves to levels ranging from 16.8 to
89.5 billion barrels. (*Petroleum Economist* 1982) Such claims,
it should be stressed, have yet to be proven and it will be
noted that most of the unexplored basins are those associated
with the arcs of recent mountain building in the region and
are considered to be of poor potential. (Figure 2.2)

The variation in estimates of oil reserves in Indonesia is
crucial for two reasons. First, although there has been a
high success rate for those wells drilled so far, most fields
discovered in the last decade are small in size and thus will
have a limited life. (Ooi 1982, 15ff) There are exceptions
such as the Attaka and Handil fields off East Kalimantan and
the Arjuna field in the northwest Java offshore basin, but
these were all relatively early finds and the implication is
that exploration must continue at a high level, and
continue to make frequent finds of new fields, if the reserve
position and production are to be maintained. Second, if the
lower figures of reserve estimates are nearer to the mark,
then it is clear that Indonesia has a mere 20-26 years of
supplies at the production levels of the late 1970s. The cutbacks of 1981-82 which reduced output to around 1.34 million
barrels per day in the latter year (488 million barrels) will
serve to extend the production period somewhat, but at the
same time domestic consumption of petroleum has been rising

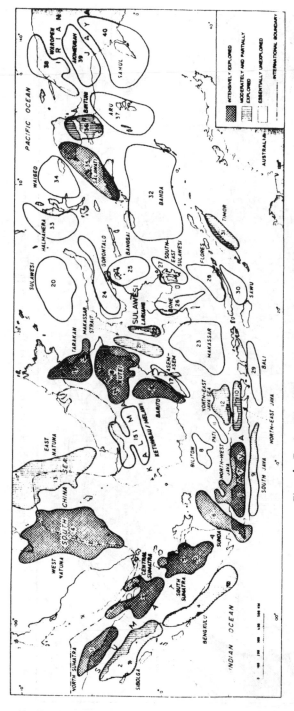

Fig. 1 Exploration status of the Tertiary basins in Indonesia

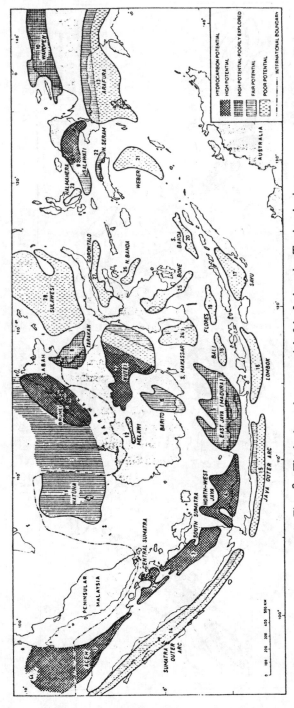

Fig. 2   The hydrocarbon potential of the Indonesian Tertiary basins

Table 2.6
Indonesia: Exports by Value 1980-82 (mn US$)

	1980	1981	1982
Live animals, animal products	219.65	213.58	243.18
inc. Shrimps	180.90	163.01	180.73
Vegetable Products	1,026.76	670.54	633.85
inc. Coffee	656.00	345.95	341.62
Tea	112.67	100.83	89.49
Pepper	50.02	47.51	45.49
Animal & Vegetable Oils	286.30	130.59	132.45
inc. Palm Oil	254.74	107.03	96.25
Prepared Foodstuffs	235.92	212.01	181.47
inc. Tobacco	58.94	50.36	37.71
Copra Cake	47.38	26.81	34.15
Bran	43.84	46.49	33.02
Sugar	22.98	17.60	13.92
Mineral Products	16,015.87	17,982.66	18,554.95
inc. Petroleum	11,671.31	13,182.06	14,001,82
Other Oil	1,178.97	1,207.66	859.57
Natural Gas	2,881.24	3,366.31	3,382.73
Copper	125.29	111.51	117.62
Tin	66.44	13.83	11.85
Chemical Industries	80.18	61.62	57.60
Artificial Resins & Plastics	1,174.69	836.20	607.85
inc. Rubber	1,069.06	828.21	602.10
Wood and Wood Articles	1,898.91	1,089.89	886.85
inc. 'Junglewood'	1,808.93	652.24	331.75
Base Metals	633.73	649.87	541.03
inc. Tin Conc.	433.64	452.11	353.24
Nickel matte	162.07	119.92	136.88
Others	336.88	413.18	452.11
TOTAL	21,908.89	22,260.34	20,284.34

Source: Bank Indonesia, *Indonesian Financial Statistics*, XVI, 12, 1983.

rapidly to eat into the country's export surplus. From a 1978 export surplus of 462 million barrels, there was a fall to just 302 million barrels in 1982 and this may decline further as new refining capacity capable of working Indonesia's low-sulphur crude has come on stream, enabling greater domestic use of the country's own supplies.(22) Petroleum consumption was heavily subsidised until January 1982 and kerosene was the main fuel even for rural areas. Prices have now been raised twice in an effort to discourage such rapid growth in consumption,(23) but it cannot be expected that Indonesia's current net balance of oil exports will long be maintained without major new discoveries.

The issue is that, to date, Indonesia has used its oil wealth mainly as a vehicle for financing investment in other sectors of the economy. The expensive rice intensification programme and the growing expenditure on transmigration, both mentioned earlier, have been made possible from oil revenues. Today the country increasingly needs its petroleum, not only for basic household and transportation use, but also for industrial purposes to support a petrochemicals industry as the base for a series of downstream manufactures of a diversified nature. These requirements mean that the days of petroleum as a major export-revenue earner must be numbered. Perhaps fortunately the developments of 1981-83 have brought the reality of the country's excessive dependence upon petroleum home to the Indonesian government in clear perspective. The OPEC-imposed production cutback has been followed by a fall in price of $5 per barrel which left Indonesia with a budget deficit for 1982-83 of an estimated US$7 billion and precipitated various measures of adjustment, including a 27 per cent devaluation of the Rupiah and major cuts in government spending. A major setback to growth in the short-term, these events have served to emphasise the need to reduce the country's dependence on oil, both in terms of its importance as a source of export earnings and investment capital *and* as a raw material and energy source. As long as oil revenues are maintained they must be used to invest in other growth sectors for the future.

Fortunately for Indonesia the cupboard is by no means bare as far as alternative resources are concerned. The scope for the expansion of cultivated area of commercial crops such as rubber and oil palm has already been mentioned. These and other crops such as coffee and tea could return to make a useful contribution to export earnings, not only as raw materials, but also in the form of secondary manufactures such as rubber goods and vegetable oil derivatives. For this,

however, there must be a continuation of investment into the
rehabilitation of these industries, particularly into the
smallholder rubber sector which still needs extensive replan-
ting and improvement of marketing facilities to improve
productivity and to make it better able to compete with
neighbouring Malaysia, now very much the world leader in the
tropical export-crop sector. As far as non-agricultural
exports are concerned there are again significant possibilities. Chief of these must be natural gas wherein must lie
the future of the Indonesian hydrocarbons industry. This has
been discovered in massive quantities in the same Tertiary
basin structures as the petroleum and already Indonesia has
taken the lead in the world in exports of gas in liquefied
form under long-term contracts to several Japanese public
utilities. Exports in 1980-81 were running at over 500
billion cubic feet, mainly from two fields at Badak in East
Kalimantan and Arun in Aceh. Plans have been laid down to
expand the level of exports to compensate for the downturn in
oil earnings, but world economic stagnation has left the
liquefied natural gas (LNG) market depressed and extremely
competitive as supplies from Malaysia, and possibly even
Thailand, in the immediate region alone, come on stream.

Nevertheless Indonesia is not considering her natural gas
resources merely in terms of a new source of foreign exchange
earnings. Already the Arun field is feeding a petrochemicals
industry centred on Lho'seumawe in Aceh, of which the first
step is a urea fertiliser plant built under the ASEAN industrial complementary scheme. Supplies are also considered
large enough to make a contribution to internal energy
requirements for the future. Reserves at the end of 1981
were put at something over 30 trillion cubic feet, but subsequently there have been reports of further discoveries in
the Natuna Sea area, which have been termed 'astronomical' and
at Lembak in South Sumatra, where an astonishing 785 trillion
cubic feet of reserves have been claimed. (*Asia Research
Bulletin* 1982, pp.5/922-23) Several sources of geothermal
energy have now been identified from volcanic areas throughout
the archipelago, and one petroleum company has now begun to
tap those in Java. On this basis, even without further oil
discoveries, with careful management Indonesia should have few
energy problems in the future.

Such resources then appear to offer Indonesia a future as a
major industrial producer and the country certainly has other
significant raw materials capable of exploitation for large-
scale industrialisation. Despite the long history of exploration, the tin resources of Bangka and Belitung appear to have

a life of thirty to forty years at current rates of working;
bauxite deposits on nearby Bintang Island are now exploited
for a new aluminium smelter on the east coast of Sumatra,
utilising the hydro-electric power from the Asahan river,
another potential energy resource in the country which remains
scarcely tapped; at the other end of the archipelago, copper
is already being worked in the Ertsberg area of Irian Jaya,
although deposits here may prove to be insignificant compared
to recent discoveries in Sumatra; in the end, indeed, the
major mineral of eastern Indonesia may prove to be nickel,
for which reserves of 824 million tonnes of ore have been
recognised in Sulawesi and at Gag Island off Irian. At
present most of these deposits are being exported with little
transformation, but as with the country's timber resources,
the Indonesian government recognises the need to link them
into a wider based industrialisation. This was demonstrated
in 1979-80 when the government made a commitment of over
US$10 billion for new large capital projects including the
petrochemicals complex, a plan to double output of LNG,
expansion of fertiliser and cement works, expansion of plywood
manufacturing capacity, the Asahan project and the Krakatau
steel works in West Java.

   This investment has been criticised by international
agencies such as the World Bank as a 'misallocation of
resources', offering little likelihood of labour absorption
in the short-term. Their suggestion is that the immediate
future of industrialisation lies in structural reforms in
relation to tariffs, laws and 'red tape', which would increase
the efficiency of labour-intensive industries and enable them
to develop an export capacity. In reply the Indonesian
government maintains that such large capital projects should
lead to a much more broadly based industrial structure for
the future. The question remains of just how far away that
future lies and whether in the shorter term the economy can
withstand the growing pressures being created by an increasing
number of people with limited economic prospects in the
Javanese heart of Indonesia. These pressures may be
intensified by the austerity measures forced upon the government by the decline in earnings from petroleum; already energy
and food subsidies have been removed, pushing up living costs
for the poor. However, decreased revenues have also forced
the government into the postponement of several of the large-
scale projects proposed and into a lower cost development
strategy such as that suggested by the World Bank with its
emphasis on employment creation. Whether this will be effective remains to be seen and events in the international
economy over the next few years are likely to be crucial to

the view of Indonesia in the late 1980s and 1990s. Renewed economic growth in the world may offer an important stimulus to the Indonesian economy and give this giant a chance to get up off her knees and fulfil her potential; continuing depression may leave the economy in the doldrums and pressures of a large population living in growing poverty may be sufficient to bring about another period of political instability which could set her back a generation.

NOTES

(1) The chapter's title derives from the paper by Fisher (1972), from whose two papers much of the introductory discussion is derived.
(2) See Introduction.
(3) Widjojo was replaced as Co-ordinating Minister for Economic Affairs by Ali Wardhana in March 1983; Wardhana had previously been Finance Minister. Widjojo retained some influence as a government advisor.
(4) May, however, views the situation of the country as having worsened as a result of Western influence since 1965.
(5) It is no accident that the Association of Southeast Asian Nations (ASEAN) was also founded in 1967; this was supported in the West in the hope of linking Indonesia economically to the essentially pro-Western governments of Malaysia, the Philippines, Singapore and Thailand.
(6) The term 'Outer Islands' or 'Outer Indonesia' refers to the country apart from Java-Madura and Bali.
(77) The degree to which the process took place has been questioned by Hayami and Kikuchi (1981, p.275).
(8) So much so that the then Governor of Jakarta, Ali Sadikin, actually closed the city to jobless migrants in 1970.
(9) Although there even is controversy over what constitutes such a minimum. See, for example, Whyte 1974.
(10) The new varieties resistant to the *wereng* were IR-36, IR-38 and the local high-yield variety Cisadano.
(11) Repelita is the Indonesian acronym for *Rencana Pembangunan Lima Tahun* (Five Year Development Plan). Repelita III is thus the third such plan, extending from 1979 to 1984.
(12) Misuse of such uplands has already caused major environmental problems in both Java and southern Sumatra.
(13) As has been the case since 1982. For further discussion see below.
(14) Although there is some controversy between the various

authorities as to whether this should be via agriculture or public works. See Arndt and Sundrum 1977; Hardjojo 1978.

(15) It must be said, however, that there are provinces of the Outer Islands which may be less prosperous than those of Java. Nusa Tenggara Barat and Nusa Tenggara Timur (the Lesser Sundas) are now recognised to have suffered from long neglect. See, for example, Esmara 1975.

(16) Normally in core-periphery models, it is the centre which is a dynamic core drawing resources from the periphery.

(17) Although some modern industries may have located just outside the boundaries of urban areas.

(18) Indonesia has been trying recently to obtain assurances from Japan that this proportion will at least be maintained.

(19) Cutbacks imposed in relation to the glut of supplies and falling free-market prices caused by the economic recession and conservation measures in major consumer countries.

(20) See Petroleum News Southeast Asia, Oil and Gas Map, January 1980.

(21) Success is defined as an exploration well which is productive of some oil and gas. Of course some of these may be non-commercial, but in these terms Indonesia's success rate in recent years has varied between 30 and 50 per cent.

(22) Until recently Indonesia's refineries have been unable to refine its own low-sulphur crude and she has imported Saudi Arabian oil for local refining. Even so refinery capacity was only adequate to supply 54 per cent of oil products consumed locally and use was made of Singapore's capacity. A major programme of refinery expansion has been under way, however, and this situation is about to change.

(23) As well as to reduce government spending on subsidies in the face of reduced revenues.

BIBLIOGRAPHY

(N.B. BIES - Bulletin of Indonesian Economic Studies, Canberra)

Arndt, H. W. 'Survey of recent developments', BIES, vol.19, no.2, 1983.

Arndt, H. W. 'Transmigration: achievements, problems, prospects', BIES, vol.19, no.3, 1983.

Arndt, H. W. and Sundrum, R. M. 'Transmigration: land settlement or regional development', BIES, vol.13, no.3, 1977.

Birowo, Achmad T. *Bimas: A Package Program for Intensifi-cation of Food Crop Production in Indonesia*, SEADAG paper on Problems of Development in Southeast Asia, Asia Society, New York, 1975.

Booth, Anne, 'Irrigation in Indonesia Part 1', *BIES*, vol.13, no.1, 1977.

Booth, Anne and McCawley, P. *The Indonesian Economy During the the Suharto Era*,,Oxford University Press, Kuala Lumpur, 1981.

Booth, Anne and Sundrum, R. M., 'Income distribution', in Booth, Anne and McCawley, P. *op. cit.*, 1981.

Cho, Lee-Jay, Suharto, S., McNicoll, G. and Made Mamas, S. G. *Population Growth of Indonesia. An Analysis of Fertility and Mortality Based on the 1971 Population Census*, University of Hawaii Press, Honolulu, 1980.

Collier, W. L. 'Food problems, unemployment and the green revolution in rural Java', *Prisma*, 9, March 1978.

Collier, W. L. 'Declining labor absorption (1878 to 1980) in Javanese rice production', *Kajian Ekonomi Malaysia*, vol.16, no.12, 1979.

Collier, W. L., Gunawan Wiradi and Soentoro, 'Recent changes in rice harvesting methods', *BIES*, vol.9, no.2, 1973.

Collier, W. L., Soentoro, Gunawan Wiradi and Makali, 'Agri-cultural technology and institutional change in Java', *Food Research Institute Studies*, vol.13, no.2, 1974.

Collier, W. L., Jusuf Colter, Sinarhadi and Shaw, R. d'A., 'Choice of technique in rice milling in Java: a comment', *BIES*, vol.10, no.1, 1974.

Collier, W. L., Soentoro, Gunawan Wiradi, Effendi Basandaran, Kabul Santoso and Stepanek, J. F., *The Acceleration of Rural Development on Java: From Village Studies to a National Perspective*, Agro-Economic Survey, Rural Dynamics Study, Occasional Paper 6, Bogor, 1983.

Dapice, D. O. 'Trends in income distribution and levels of living' in Papanek, G. F., *op. cit.*, 1980.

Esmara, Hendra, 'Regional income disparities', *BIES*, vol.11, no.1, 1975.

Fisher, C. A. 'Economic myth and geographical reality in Indonesia', *Modern Asian Studies*, vol.1, no.2, 1967.

Fisher, C. A. 'Indonesia - a giant astir', *Geographical Journal*, vol..138, no.2, 1972.

Geertz, Clifford, *Agricultural Involution. The Process of Ecological Change in Indonesia*, University of California Press, Berkeley, 1963.

Glassburner, B. and Poffenberger, M. 'Survey of recent devel-opments', *BIES*, vol.19, no.3, 1983.

Hanna, W. A. *Bung Karno's Indonesia*, American Universities Field Staff Reports Service, Southeast Asia Series, New York, 1961.

Hanson, A. J. 'Transmigration, and marginal land development' in Hansen, G. E. (ed.), *Agricultural and Rural Development in Indonesia*, Westview, Boulder, Colorado, 1981.

Hardjono, J. M. *Transmigration in Indonesia*, OOxford University Press, Kuala Lumpur, 1977.

Hardjono, J. M. 'Transmigration: a new concept?', *BIES*, vol.14, no.1, 1978.

Hayami, Y. and Hafed, A. 'Rice harvesting and welfare in rural Java', *BIES*, vol.15, no.2, 1979.

Hayami, Y. and Kikuchi, M. *Asian Village Economy at the Crossroad. An Economic Approach to Institutional Change*, University of Tokyo Press, Tokyo, 1981.

Hugo, G. J. 'Migration to and from Jakarta' in Pryor, R. J. (ed.), *Migration and Development in South-East Asia*, Oxford University Press, Kuala Lumpur, 1979.

Hull, T. H. 'Rapid fertility decline. A comment', *BIES*, vol.12, no.2, 1976.

Hull, T. H. 'Fertility decline in Indonesia. A review of recent evidence', *BIES*, vol.16, no.2, 1980.

Hull, T. H. 'Indonesia's population growth 1971-80', *BIES*, vol.17, no.1, 1981.

Hull, T. H. and Mantra, I. B. 'Indonesia's changing population' in Booth, Anne and McCawley, P. *op. cit.*, 1981.

Ihalauw, J. and Widya Utami, 'Klaten, Central Java' in International Rice Research Institute, *Changes in Rice Farming in Selected Areas of Asia*, IRRI, Los Banos, 1975.

Indonesia, Biro Pusat Statistik, *Sensus Pertanian 1973. Jilid 1*, Jakarta, 1976.

Krausse, G. H. 'Intra-urban variations in Kampung settlements in Jakarta. A structural analysis', *Journal of Tropical Geography*, vol.46, 1978.

Laquian, A. A. 'Squatters and slum dwellers' in Yeh, S. H. K. and Laquian, A. A. *Housing Asia's Millions: Problems, Policies and Prospects For Low-Cost Housing in Southeast Asia*, IDRC, Ottawa, 1979.

Lingard, J. and Al Sri Bagyo, 'The impact of agricultural mechanisation on production and employment in rice areas of West Java', *BIES*, vol.19, no.1, 1983.

Lingard, J. and Wicks, J. A. 'Impact of mechanising small scale rice production in the Philippines, Indonesia and Thailand: Some empirical evidence', in Greenshields, B. L. and Bellamy, M. A. (eds), *Rural Development: Growth and Equity*, Gower, Aldershot, 1983.

Luthy, Herbert, 'Indonesia confronted. Part 1', *Encounter*, December 1965.

McCawley, Peter, 'Survey of recent developments', *BIES*, vol.19, no.1, 1983.

McGee, T. G. *Hawkers in Hong Kong: A Study of Planning and*

Policy in a Third World City, Hong Kong, 1973.

May, Brian, *The Indonesian Tragedy,* Routledge & Kegan Paul, London, 1978.

Mears, L. A. 'A new approach to rice intensification', *BIES,* vol.6, no.2, 1970.

Mears, L. A. and Sidik Moeljono, 'Food policy', in Booth, Anne and Mc. Cawley, P. *op. cit.,* 1981.

Metzner, J. K. *Agriculture and Population Pressure in Sikka, Isle of Flores,* Australian National University, Development Studies Centre Monograph no.28, Canberra, 1982.

Ooi, Jin-Bee, *The Petroleum Resources of Indonesia,* Oxford University Press, Kuala Lumpur, 1982.

Papanek, G. F. (ed.) *The Indonesian Economy,* Praeger, New York, 1980.

Poot, H. 'The development of labour intensive industries in Indonesia' in Rashid Amjad, (ed.), *The Development of Labour Intensive Industries in ASEAN Countries,* ILO, Bangkok, 1981.

Prabowo, Dibyo and Sajogyo, 'Sidoarjo, East Java and Subang, West Java' in International Rice Research Institute, *Changes in Rice Farming in Selected Areas of Asia,* Las Banos, 1975.

Sadli, M. 'Indonesia's experience with the application of technology and its employment effects', *Ekonomi dan Keuangan Indonesia,* vol.3, 1973.

Sajogyo, *Modernisation without Development in Rural Java,* Bogor Agricultural Institute, Bogor, 1972.

Sajogyo, *Usaha Perbaikan Gizi Keluarga: ANP Evaluation Study,* Bogor Agricultural Institute, Bogor, 1975 (quoted in Booth, Anne and Sundrum, R. M. *op. cit.,* 1981).

Sinaga, R. 'Implications of agricultural mechanisation for employment and income distributions', *BIES,* vol.14, no.2, 1978.

Sinaga, R. *The Effect of Mechanisation on Productivity in West Java',* Consequences of Mechanisation Working Paper 1, IRRI, Los Banos, 1981.

Sinaga, R. *The Effect of Mechanisation on Productivity in South Sulawesi,* Consequences of Mechanisation Working Paper 42, IRRI, Los Banos, 1981.

Specter, M. 'A sprawling, thirsty giant', *Far Eastern Economic Review,* vol.123, no.13, 1984.

Sundrum, R. M. 'Income distribution 1970-76', *BIES,* vol.15, no.1, 1979.

Suratman and Guinness, P. 'The changing focus of transmigration', *BIES,* vol.13, no.2, 1977.

Timmer, C. P. 'Choice of technique in rice milling in Java', *BIES,* vol.9, no.2, 1973.

Timmer, C. P. 'Choice of technique in rice milling. A reply',

BIES, vol.10, no.1, 1974.

Utomo, Kampto, 'Villages of unplanned resettlers in the sub-district Kaliredjo, Central Lampung' in Koenjaraningrat (ed.), *Villages in Indonesia*, Cornell University Press, Ithaca, 1967.

van Ginneken, W. *Rural and Urban Income Inequalities in Indonesia, Mexico, Pakistan, Tanzania and Tunisia*, ILO, Geneva, 1976.

Whyte, R. O. *Rural Nutrition in Monsoon Asia*, Oxford University Press, Kuala Lumpur, 1974.

World Bank, *Indonesia Irrigation Program Review*, Washington, 1978.

3 Industrial development and trade

JOHN WALTON

Despite Indonesia's wealth of natural resources, discussed in the preceding article by Dr. Demaine, average *per capita* income is low, estimated by the World Bank to be US$530 in 1981. To understand why such a potentially rich country remains relatively poor after more than thirty years of independence it is necessary to look back briefly on its recent history.

From 1958, under 'Guided Democracy', nationalist and political ideals assumed more or less complete ascendancy over economic rationale. The several armed conflicts over territorial disputes of the time, outlined in the Introduction, resulted in large military expenditures which placed a severe strain upon the economy. This was probably one of the key factors in the ensuing hyper-inflation which in 1966 reached an annual rate of 650 per cent. The period witnessed a large scale take-over of foreign firms: Dutch plantations and mining enterprises as a result of the West Irian dispute, and United States and European firms when Indonesia failed to gain support for its confrontation policy with Malaysia.

The disruption following nationalisation, and government expenditure on non-productive prestigious projects, created further economic chaos with growth of national output slowing to an annual average of about one per cent during the 1960-66

43

period. With population increasing at almost three per cent per annum, this meant that per capita income actually declined in this period, although the consequences were somewhat mitigated because the mass of population remained within the subsistence sector, and there was also some subsidisation of basic needs in the urban areas.

This unfortunate period came to an end with the allegedly communist-inspired abortive *coup d'état* in late 1965, which gave the army the opportunity to ease Sukarno out of office and establish a 'New Order' under General Suharto. With the economy in almost total collapse, Suharto faced the daunting task of restoring economic and political stability. The legacy he inherited included:

1. Inflation at 650 per cent per annum.
2. External debts in excess of US$2 billion.
3. Transportation and communications nearly at a standstill.
4. Production capacities in major industries at extremely low levels due to shortage of imported materials and spare parts.
5. Economic and political instability.

From 1966 under his direction a new strategy was followed, with the emphasis on development. The first priority was to re-establish some economic stability and this was achieved with remarkable speed as the inflation rate dropped to 120 per cent in 1967, 85 per cent in 1968 and 10 per cent in 1969. Internally this was accomplished by a sharp reduction in government expenditure, especially the cancellation of prestigious and grandiose projects, the introduction of tight monetary controls and strict adherence to a balanced budget. In addition efforts were made to improve tax collection. Indonesia's return to a system whereby resources were allocated by the market mechanism received favourable backing from the West, which rescheduled outstanding debts and provided substantial credits. American food shipments together with rehabilitation of the rice sector helped to stabilise rice prices, which proved to be a crucial factor in reducing the rate of inflation.

In 1967, to reaffirm the change in economic strategy, it was announced that compensation would be paid to enterprises nationalised under the Sukarno administration, and new legislation was introduced to attract both foreign and domestic capital. The period up to 1969 can best be described as one of rehabilitation when the major focus was the elimination of supply bottlenecks in essential industries and the stabilisation of the economy.

The return to a more normal economy by late 1968 enabled the
government to devote greater attention to development objectives and in 1969 it launched the first of a series of five-
year plans - Repelita I (1969-74). Its major emphasis was
directed at rehabilitation of the economy, rather than the
initiation of new projects. The main objectives were greatly
increased rice production and reconstruction of the infrastructure, especially irrigation and transportation. This was
reflected in the allocation of development expenditure, which
was channelled largely towards transportation, communication,
agriculture, irrigation and fertiliser subsidies. The
expansion of rice production was singled out as the most
important priority because of its central role in achieving
economic stability. The goal of self-sufficiency through a
fifty per cent increase in rice production within the plan
period was rather ambitious and actual performance approximately a twenty-five per cent increase, fell well below target.
Today, ten years later, the goal of self-sufficiency still
remains elusive.

On the industrial side, several basic industries were
selected for special attention and were underpinned by public
investment. These included fertilisers, cement, chemicals,
and pulp and paper, whilst little priority was accorded to
small-scale industries. However the foreign investment
legislation enacted prior to the plan in 1967 encouraged a
substantial inflow of foreign private capital into the
extractive industries including petroleum, minerals and timber.
The period also witnessed heightened activity by both foreign
and domestic investors in the import-substituting industries
such as light manufacturing, including textiles and food
processing.

Given the economic disruption of the 1960s, Indonesia
achieved considerable success within the 1969-74 plan period.
Real GDP increased on average by over seven per cent per
annum, and several run-down industries and areas of infrastructure were successfully brought back to economic service.
Most production targets were realised apart from rice as
already mentioned. There was a shortfall in anticipated public
development expenditure, although this was to some extent offset by the inflow of foreign capital which not only improved
the balance of payments situation but also helped to raise
gross domestic investment from twelve per cent of GDP in 1969
to eighteen per cent by the end of the plan period in 1974.

The Second Five Year Plan - Repelita II (1974-79) broadly
followed the objectives introduced in the previous plan. The

basic economic policies and sectoral development priorities
remained largely unchanged, but there was some re-ordering of
emphasis in relation to social welfare. Employment, education,
health and family planning assumed greater importance and
received more financial support. Nevertheless agriculture,
irrigation, transport and communications and regional development remained the leading sectors for development expenditure.

Continuing on the foundations laid by Repelita I, the Second
Five Year Plan came into force in 1974, when Indonesia's
economy was to be significantly affected by both external and
internal factors. The major foreign influence was the quad-
rupling of oil prices associated with the OPEC crisis of
1973-74, which gave a dramatic boost to Indonesia's foreign
exchange earnings, already substantially greater as a result
of oil production increases from 0.5 million barrels per day
in 1969 to 1.5 million barrels per day in 1974, in response to
large inflows of foreign investment encouraged by the growing
rationalisation of the economy under the Suharto
administration.

Substantially increased foreign exchange reserves created
opportunities for development expenditure considerably in
excess of that originally envisaged in Repelita II, but
initial optimism was dampened by the onset of the 1975 crisis
of Pertamina, the state oil corporation. Under the leadership
of General Sutowo, it had established what amounted to a
parallel economy not accountable to the government, and
indulged in several ill-advised prestigious projects financed
by devious loans. In essence short term borrowing through a
roll over process was used to finance long term capital intensive projects. However in February and March 1975 Pertamina
was unable to repay, on time, short term loans totalling
US$100 million to a consortium of American and Canadian banks
which prompted the government, through Bank Indonesia, to
assume responsibility for Pertamina's debts. Although total
debts were not officially disclosed, if onerous contractual
commitments such as the hire-purchase of oil tankers are
included, it came to light that total debts were probably in
the region of US$10 billion, which in practice soaked up most
of Indonesia's newly inflated foreign exchange reserves
during 1976.

Despite the Pertamina problem, government expenditure during
Repelita II was in fact considerably higher than originally
planned, and in most sectors actual performance was only
marginally lower than the projected rates of growth. Overall
GDP was expected to increase at 7.5 per cent per annum, and

with an estimated population growth of 2.3 per cent, per capita GDP was therefore to grow at 5.2 per cent. In practice real GDP averaged 6.8 per cent, and per capita GDP averaged 4.7 per cent per annum.

The Third Five Year Plan - Repelita III (1979-84) - was introduced as a development trilogy of economic growth, equitable distribution of development benefits, and political and economic stability. The target rate of real GDP was set at 6.5 per cent per annum, compared to 7.5 per cent for Repelita II, the lower rate partly reflecting some sacrifice of growth for more ambitious social goals, but also in anticipation of slower growth in the agricultural sector (3.5 per cent per annum) and the mining sector (4 per cent per annum). The industrial sector with an expected growth rate of 11 per cent per annum still retained its position as the leading sector, closely followed by transport and communications, with a projected annual growth rate of 10 per cent. The introduction of Repelita III, like its predecessor, coincided with unexpected oil price increases which whilst initially, and beneficially, bolstering foreign exchange reserves, set the scene for depressed world economic activity and the eventual collapse of oil prices in 1983, while the imposition of production quotas by OPEC placed severe constraints on Indonesia's development objectives. In addition non-oil trade also suffered adversely as a consequence of reduced world demand.

Tables 3.1, 3.2 and 3.3 indicate some of the major structural changes and growth rates experienced over the last two decades.

Table 3.1 shows a diminution in the share of agriculture as the rapid growth of the oil industry increased the importance of the industrial sector. Manufacturing, however, remains a relatively small component, especially if compared with other countries of ASEAN, for instance 25 per cent in the Philippines, 20 per cent in Thailand and 18 per cent in Malaysia. As usual, the service sector expanded in response to increased industrial activity.

Table 3.2 shows a noticeable change in the composition of the labour force as employment opportunities increased in the secondary and tertiary sectors. Agriculture remains the major employment sector and is not significantly different from the situation in Malaysia and the Philippines where agricultural employment accounts respectively for 50 per cent and 46 per cent of the total labour force. Compared with Thailand, where 76 per cent of the labour force remains in the agricultural

Table 3.1
Structure of Production, 1960-81
(as percentage of GDP)

	1960	1981
Agriculture	50	24
Industry	25	42
(Manufacturing	(8)	(12)
Services	25	34
	100	100

Source: World Development Reports 1982-83

Table 3.2
Structure of Labour Force, 1960-80
(percentages)

	1960	1980
Agriculture	75	55
Industry	8	15
Services	17	30
	100	100

Source: World Development Report 1983

Table 3.3
Growth of Production
Average Annual Growth Rates 1960-70 & 1970-81
(percentages)

	1960-70	1970-81
GDP	3.9	7.8
Agriculture	2.7	3.8
Industry	5.2	11.2
Manufacturing	3.3	13.9
Services	4.8	9.5

Source: World Development Report 1983

sector, Indonesia has experienced considerable structural change

Table 3.3 clearly indicates the heightened economic activity of the 1970s in contrast to the dismal performance of the 1960s. Growth rates in the 1970s compare well internationally, although that for agriculture is somewhat lower than experienced elsewhere in South-East Asia. Overall, recent economic growth suggests that the Suharto administration, following relatively conventional and rational economic development strategies, has achieved considerable success in rescuing the country from economic collapse and steering it along a reasonably stable growth path. However, to understand some of the more basic problems facing the Indonesian economy, a closer examination of the structure of industry and trade is required if we are to evaluate the implications of government policies in relation to these important areas of the economy.

INDUSTRIAL STRUCTURE

Indonesia's economy is primarily based on dualistic agriculture and extractive industry, although recent development policy has stimulated manufacturing growth. The majority of Indonesia's labour force is employed in smallholder agriculture producing food crops, especially rice, for domestic consumption, or cash crops such as rubber for export. Estate agriculture consists of rubber, palm oil, coconuts, coffee and other tropical crops produced mainly for export. In a low income economy and highly populated country such as Indonesia, the importance of food production should not be underestimated, since food accounts for approximately half of consumer incomes.(1) The government logistics board - BULOG - has over recent years imported vast quantities of rice to stabilise domestic prices and restrain inflationary trends, and though successful the implementation of this policy has incurred a fairly high foreign exchange cost which Indonesia can ill afford to maintain in a deteriorating balance of payments situation.

The agricultural export sector has been neglected if compared with neighbouring Malaysia, perhaps to some extent because of the over reliance on oil revenues. However, uncertainty over oil prices has led to increased awareness of the need to diversify the export base, and more attention is now being directed to this sector. Timber also forms an important division of agriculture but export revenues are now lower due to the government's decision to ban log exports in order to develop the wood-processing industry, especially plywood manufacture.

Despite recent problems associated with the world oil market, by far the most important part of the Indonesian economy is the petroleum and natural gas industry. This accounts for 70-80 per cent of total commodity exports and over 60 per cent of government revenue. It is this sector which, benefiting from multiple price increases since 1973, has provided the major financial resources for the implementation of development projects. Pertamina is responsible for all oil and natural gas activities including exploration, production and refining, transportation and marketing. However, most development activity is carried out by foreign oil companies, serving as production-sharing contractors with Pertamina.

These agreements have tended to follow a standard formula, which requires the contractor to bear all exploration and production costs, although these are recoverable from the oil produced. The production-sharing ratio is 85:15 for oil and 70:30 for natural gas in favour of Pertamina. Contractors are required to sell 10 per cent of their interest to an Indonesian company if oil is discovered in commercial quantities. They must also allocate part of their share of production for domestic use which is sold to Pertamina at cost plus US$0.20 per barrel, starting from the sixth year of production. Contractors must process 28.5 per cent of their share of production in Indonesia, and may be required to build refining facilities or petrochemical plants if existing capacity is insufficient. The main exception to the above formula has been the contract-of-work agreements with Caltex and Stanvac, negotiated prior to 1967. These twenty-year contracts, essentially profit-sharing, expired in November 1983 and Caltex has recently signed a production-sharing agreement closely following the standard formula, although the ratio now becomes 88:12 in favour of Pertamina. Moreover Caltex is required to invest US$3.06 billion within the first ten years of the new eighteen-year contract, otherwise Pertamina will impose a 95:5 split as compensation.(2) Caltex, jointly owned by Standard Oil of California and Texaco, was the first oil company to establish production facilities in Indonesia and accounts for over half of the country's total oil production from its concessions in Sumatra. Pertamina could probably exact more onerous contracts but the nature of Indonesian oil deposits, generally small and fragmented, requires continued exploration activity if high levels of production are to be maintained. Too onerous contracts would deter potential investors.

In face of declining demand and falling prices Indonesia reduced production in 1982 to 1.3 million barrels per day from 1.6 million in 1981, and both production and exports fell by about 17 per cent. The fall in petroleum revenues and the uncertainty concerning oil prices have caused the government to moderate its development expenditure, though increased exports of natural gas have helped to avert a potentially serious situation.

Despite the slowdown in production there has been increased activity on the exploration side. In 1981 there were twelve production-sharing agreements signed, with thirteen in 1982. The number of exploration wells doubled from 160 in 1980 to 320 in 1982; thus a high level of interest is being maintained.

MANUFACTURING

Manufacturing has grown at approximately 13 per cent per annum since 1970 and is one of the most rapidly expanding sectors of the economy. It has steadily increased its share of GDP from 8 per cent in the 1960s to 12 per cent in 1981. Before 1966, as a result of political and economic instability, the manu- facturing sector remained small, backward and under-developed, and it was not until after the austerity and rehabilitation measures of the late 1960s that manufacturing was able to assume a dynamic role in the Indonesian economy, suitably encouraged by stimulating investment conditions and also, despite relatively low incomes, a pent-up demand due to the long period of shortages prior to 1970. Not surprisingly, many opportunities arose for import-substituting industries and these generated the initial impetus for the growth of the manufacturing sector. Although it is dominated by light consumer-goods industries, mainly processing agricultural products, considerable diversification has taken place over the last fifteen years, with the growth of basic industries leading towards a more balanced industrial sector. Heavy industries such as cement, fertilisers, petrochemicals and basic metals, all predominantly state-owned, have been responsible for the rapid rise of manufacturing. Growth has been primarily in response to major construction projects financed by the oil price windfall, including the building of schools, hospitals, offices, factories, transport and communications networks. However, the heavy industries, whilst generating high value- added, are highly capital-intensive, and most employment opportunities have arisen in the smaller establishments of the light consumer goods sector, especially cottage industries. Indeed the diverse constituency of Indonesian manufacturing in

51

some ways exhibits a dualistic structure similar to that of agriculture in the sense that a relatively small number of medium to large scale firms, approximately 7,000, generate 80 per cent of manufacturing value-added whilst employing only 13 per cent of the workforce. On the other hand, the unorganised cottage industries account for 80 per cent of manufacturing employment, but generate only 13 per cent of value-added. A clearer perception of the structure of manufacturing can be gleaned by examining its organised and unorganised parts in more detail from data made available by the 1974 industrial census.(3)

The unorganised sector comprises household or cottage industries which are primarily rural-based and employ less than five workers. It is estimated that about four million workers, or 80 per cent of the total manufacturing workforce, are employed in 1.3 million establishments, mainly producing food and beverages, which account for 44 per cent of value-added for this group. Other important activities include the processing of wood and its products, especially bamboo and rattan, and the manufacture of textiles, bricks and tiles. Although responsible for most of the employment in Indonesian manufacturing, these establishments often provide only part-time employment, with at least a third of the workers so engaged. Productivity is extremely low with yearly value-added amounting to less than US$50 per worker.

The organised sector comprises small, medium and large scale enterprises. Small establishments, approximately 50,000 and classified as 5-19 workers, employ about one third of a million people producing goods similar to the cottage industries, but productivity is higher with value-added per worker averaging US$300 in 1974. Small industries employ 7 per cent of manufacturing's workforce, and generate the same proportion of its value-added.

In the medium scale establishments (20-99 workers) food and textiles still predominate, although there is a greater degree of sophistication in production processes with the use of modern equipment. According to the 1974 industrial census there were 5,653 medium scale enterprises employing 221,000 workers giving an average of 39 employees each.

Large scale enterprises, 100 employees or more, totalled 1,301 in 1974 with an average workforce of 370. The large and medium scale industries can be conveniently grouped together under the nomenclature of modern industry, even though traditional industries such as food, tobacco, sugar, rubber and textiles still form its main base. Nevertheless, value-added per worker in 1974 averaged just over US$1,700 or almost forty times greater than in the cottage industries. The modern enterprises are urban-based and heavily concentrated in Java, where 85 per cent are located. Moreover, this region also accounts for 75 per cent of cottage industries and highlights the hegemonic position of Java within the Indonesian economy.

Table 3.4 indicates the structure of ownership of medium and large scale establishments. This shows private domestic firms accounting for 88 per cent of the total number of establishments employing 70 per cent of the labour force, but producing only 54 per cent of the value-added. In contrast government and foreign enterprises account for only 12 per cent of the number of establishments, but generate 46 per cent of value-added, using 30 per cent of the labour force. On average foreign firms are more than twice the size of domestic private firms, whilst government enterprises are three times larger in terms of employment. These data clearly reflect the larger capital-intensive nature of the government and foreign enterprises.

Table 3.4
Ownership - Medium and Large Firms
(percentages)

	Private Domestic	Government	Foreign
Number of Establishments	88	8	4
Output	59	20	21
Value added	54	23	23
Employment	70	20	10
Average size Employees per firm	80	275	175

Source: Industrial Census 1974

TRADE

Over recent years oil and natural gas have accounted for 70-80 per cent of total export receipts and will continue to dominate external trade for some time, despite the recent disruption of oil markets. The major components of Indonesia's exports and imports are shown in Tables 3.5 and 3.6.

Table 3.5
Exports 1981

	US$ million	as % of total
Crude oil & oil products	14,391	64.6
Liquefied natural gas (LNG)	3,366	15.0
Timber and wood products	883	4.0
Rubber	835	3.8
Tin	441	2.0
Coffee	347	1.5
Fish & fish products	203	0.9
Other	1,793	8.1
Total	22,260	100.0

Source: Indonesia Development News 5, 9, May 1982, p.3.

Table 3.6
Imports 1981

	US$ million	as % of total
Machinery & Equipment	3,030	22.8
Oil fuels	1,730	13.0
Iron and steel goods	1,470	11.1
Motor Vehicles	1,240	9.3
Sugar & confectioneries	583	4.4
Organic chemicals	464	3.5
Synthetic resins & plastics	419	3.2
Other	4,334	32.7
Total	13,270	100.0

Source: *Ibid.*

Indonesia's trade is essentially the exchange of primary products for manufactured goods. In 1980 primary products accounted for 97 per cent of merchandise exports, whilst machinery and transport equipment and other manufactures made up 67 per cent of imports. This pattern is likely to remain unchanged for some considerable time as Indonesia continues to import large quantities of capital goods to support industrial development projects.

The destination of exports is shown in Table 3.7 and the origin of imports in Table 3.8.

Table 3.7
Destination of Exports – 1981

	US$ million	as % of total
Japan	10,540	47.3
USA	4,080	18.3
Singapore	2,170	9.7
Trinidad	896	4.0
Bahamas	825	3.7
Australia	447	2.0
Philippines	411	1.8
Other countries	2,891	13.0
Total	22,260	100.0

Source: *Ibid.*

Table 3.8
Origin of Imports – 1981

	US$ million	as % of total
Japan	3,900	30.1
USA	1,800	13.6
Singapore	1,240	9.3
West Germany	904	6.8
Saudi Arabia	671	5.1
United Kingdom	546	4.1
South Korea	488	3.7
Taiwan	400	3.0
Australia	362	2.7
Other countries	2,959	22.3
Total	13,270	100.0

Source: *Ibid.*

Eighty per cent of Indonesia's export trade is directed to industrial market economies with a further 19 per cent to other developing countries. Only one per cent is destined for non-market economies. Japan is by far the major trading partner in terms of both exports and imports, with the United States a poor second.

TRADE AND INDUSTRY - POLICIES

The structure of industry and trade outlined above clearly
demonstrates major imbalances within these sectors. Despite
the government's expressed desire to effect structural change,
imbalances still persist and prove difficult to modify and it
appears that some policies relating to trade and industry have
actually inhibited change.

Indonesian trade and industry was controlled and directed by
an extremely large diversity of incentives and regulations,
many of which have been formulated on an ad hoc basis as crises
or problems arose within individual sectors. As a result an
unwieldy system has evolved which often militates against
efficiency and growth. The system became exceedingly complex
in the period following Sukarno, when the domestic market
provided attractive opportunities for import-substituting
industries to establish themselves and request preferential
treatment whilst, given the strength of the oil sector,
pressures to develop non-oil exports were minimal. Numerous
price and non-price interventions including a variety of taxes,
customs duties, import and export quotas, subsidies, exemp-
tions, certificates, rebates and licences, etc., have
culminated in a situation whereby a strong bias and effective
protection have emerged in favour of import-substituting
industries, whilst in the case of some export-oriented
industries negative protection may be apparent, i.e. a positive
disincentive to export.

Because of the multitude of regulations, often ill-defined
and ambiguous, the scope for corruption and illegal payments
is greatly enhanced and frequent criticism has been voiced
regarding the cumbersome nature of the regulatory system. For
instance a World Bank report published in 1981 quotes the case
of an importer required to go through eighty-eight steps to
clear goods through customs.(4) The report goes on to conclude
that the regulatory environment imposes a high social cost,
that Indonesia can ill afford to carry, by its discouragement
of risk taking and long term investments in favour of quick-
yielding high-profit activities.

The problems associated with a heavy bias towards import-
substitution are well known and have been experienced in
several countries. The considerable degree of protection and
lack of competing imports allow high-cost industries to emerge
which are unable to compete in international markets. Further-

more industries may be established which misallocate domestic resources, thus comparative advantage may be ignored in favour of less appropriate industries, especially those of a capital-intensive nature. The ensuing economic structure lacks balance and is inefficient and eventually leads to stagnation. Although the Indonesian industrial sector has not reached that point, the problems noted above are apparent and will become worse unless industrial and trade policies are rationalised. Up to the present, the opportunities for industrial expansion have been provided by the domestic market. However, in most industries the relatively easy opportunities for import substitution have been exhausted and further growth and deepening of the industrial base will depend to a larger extent on export promotion, despite the large size of Indonesia's population. Compared to other South-East Asian countries Indonesia's manufacturing exports account for only 3 per cent of total exports, whereas the shares for Malaysia, Thailand and the Philippines were, in 1981, 19 per cent, 29 per cent and 37 per cent respectively.

FOREIGN INVESTMENT

Since the Suharto administration came to power foreign investment has been pursued vigorously. Between 1967 and 1983 over 800 projects with an investment commitment of over US$14 billion were approved by the Investment Co-ordinating Board (BKPM). This does not include oil, gas, banking and insurance which are classified separately.

From Table 3.9 it can be seen that the major foreign investment commitments have been in the manufacturing sector, especially metals, chemicals and textiles.

Table 3.10 clearly indicates Japan as the most important source of investment, accounting for 35 per cent of total commitment, whilst the United States and Hong Kong each account for 8 per cent.

Three quarters of the total number of projects, amounting to 59 per cent of total investment commitment, are located in Java. Projects are typically capital-intensive and create only limited employment opportunities.

Initial policy towards foreign investment displayed a liberal attitude within a framework of generous incentives and few limitations. However, since 1974 a more restrictive attitude has prevailed, possibly as a consequence of public concern at

Table 3.9
Foreign Investment Approvals by Sector 1967–83

Sector	Projects	Investment Commitment (US$ million)
Agriculture	53	266.4
Forestry	57	499.0
Fishery	27	170.0
Mining	12	1,497.3
Food Industry	49	455.9
Textiles	62	1,249.0
Wood	20	258.5
Paper	18	859.2
Chemicals	133	2,183.5
Nonferrous minerals	26	753.2
Basic metals	19	2,806.4
Metal products	160	2,154.7
Other industries	15	37.0
Construction	72	177.4
Hotels	10	297.9
Real estate	6	61.0
Transportation	16	117.8
Trade services	34	469.2
Other services	20	102.9
Total	809	14,416.3

Source: BKPM

Table 3.10
Foreign Investment Approval by Country of Origin 1967–83

Country	Projects	Investment Commitment (US$ million)
Japan	210	4,999.5
United States	74	1,172.8
Hong Kong	127	1,143.8
Belgium	15	896.2
Canada	5	863.3
Holland	42	630.3
West Germany	25	394.7
United Kingdom	51	360.0
The Philippines	12	281.1
Switzerland	20	246.4
Australia	35	214.3
India	12	193.0
Singapore	31	170.7
South Korea	15	150.7
Panama	9	127.5
Taiwan	3	122.5
Other countries	123	2,449.5
Total	809	14,416.3

Source: BKPM

foreign economic domination (which culminated in the anti-Japanese riots of 1974), but also perhaps increased oil revenues allowed nationalistic aspirations to carry more weight. Controls were imposed excluding foreign investment from specified areas such as distribution and telecommunications, but the most significant change required Indonesian equity participation in the form of joint-ventures, initially at 20 per cent but to be increased to a minimum of 51 per cent within ten years. Though additional incentives are available for export oriented investment and projects located outside of Java, the cumbersome and complex regulatory and licensing system associated with BKPM (the body controlling investment), and through which all foreign investment must be channeled, tends to be counterproductive by negating the incentive effect. (Indeed, in the domestic sector, where private investors are not necessarily committed to BKPM, many prefer to forego potential incentives on the assumption that they are outweighed by simpler procedures and lack of bureaucratic controls.) The result of the changed investment climate was a reversal of the previous rising trend of foreign investment. This peaked at about US$600 million in 1974, declining to about US$300 million in 1979.(5) It also appears that foreign investment of recent origin is more likely to be associated with already established enterprises which have mastered (perhaps at considerable cost) the complexities of the regulatory system, rather than with new entrants into Indonesia.

THE ECONOMY IN THE 1980s

In the current decade the Indonesian economy has experienced quite dramatic changes. Initially, as mentioned previously, the increased oil prices in 1979 bade well for Indonesia by augmenting foreign exchange earnings. However, the euphoria was cut short when the world economy slumped, partly as a consequence of those prices. The reduced demand for oil eventually forced crude down from US$34 to US$29 per barrel in March 1983, and Indonesia's economy, so heavily reliant upon oil, found itself facing serious balance of payments problems. Without question the revenue from oil has been, and will continue to be, extremely advantageous for Indonesia's economic growth, by providing investment funds for other key areas of the economy, and stimulating linkage and multiplier effects. Set against such obvious benefits, however, it is necessary to recognise some of the associated problems.

Based upon oil wealth, and despite inflationary tendencies, the rupiah since the mid-1970s has generally been regarded as a relatively strong currency, and as such has made export promotion more difficult in the non-oil sectors. Perhaps even more damaging, but difficult to quantify, is that the 'easy source of income' syndrome associated with oil wealth created an economic climate which either induced undesirable distortions and imbalances within the economy, or prevented or delayed the reform of existing constraints upon growth and efficiency. The return to a less buoyant economy has permitted the government to embark on a series of reforms which, if effectively implemented, should result in a more balanced economic structure by stimulating faster growth in the non-oil sector.

Even before the present recession, the government demonstrated its concern over the poor export performance of the non-oil sector by devaluing the rupiah by 50 per cent in November 1978. It should be noted that this decision was not preceded by the usual situation of a deteriorating balance of payments or dwindling foreign exchange reserves. On the contrary, the latter, because of oil revenues, were quite substantial at around US$2.5 billion.

The immediate response to devaluation was, in percentage terms, a large increase in many non-oil exports. However, in absolute terms the increases were modest, but nevertheless beneficial, because original export-base figures were extremely low. Furthermore, the increases were largely accomplished through the use of excess capacity in existing industries, rather than through new investment or structural change. This to some extent would have been inhibited by the restrictive regulatory system already discussed. Also, inflation rates in Indonesia, somewhat higher than those of its major trading partners, subsequently blunted the competitive edge gained from the devaluation. Yet another factor reducing its impact was the 1978-79 oil price increases. They stimulated a domestic boom, underpinned by policies which were heavily biased in favour of production for the domestic market, and once again the buoyancy of home demand reduced pressures to concentrate on non-oil exports.

In January 1982 Indonesia introduced new measures to stimulate non-oil exports including counter-trade agreements. This policy requires foreign suppliers to purchase Indonesian non-oil products equivalent to the value of equipment and/or materials they supply primarily in connection with government contracts in excess of US$750,000.

Due to both the fall in demand for oil and the international

recession, Indonesia's balance of payments, in surplus on
current account by US$2 billion in 1980/81, turned to a
deficit of almost US$3 billion in 1981/82, and US$6.7 billion
in 1982/83. Although foreign exchange reserves amounted to
US$10 billion at the beginning of 1982, and could be run down
to cushion partly the effects of the balance of payments
deficit, its magnitude required firm action. The main
response in March 1983 was a 28 per cent devaluation which set
an exchange rate of Rp 970 to the US$. This effectively
curbed a drain on the reserves, caused by a large speculative
capital flight anticipating devaluation. To reduce public
expenditure and slow down imports of capital goods, the government announced the postponement of four major projects
representing a saving of US$ 5 billion. These were the
US$1.35 billion Musi oil refinery in South Sumatra, two petro-
chemical plants at Plaju and Aceh, each projected to cost
US$1.5 billion, and the US$600 million alumina project at
Bintang. Other measures included a freeze on wages in the
public sector and a drastic reduction in domestic fuel subsidies. Between 1974 and 1982 domestic oil consumption
increased from 67.9 million barrels to 158.8 million barrels
per annum, representing an average annual increase of 11 per
cent, and raising the share of total production absorbed by
the home market from 13.5 per cent to 32.5 per cent.(6)
Reduced subsidies and higher fuel prices should help to
correct price distortions within the energy sector, and
promote more efficiency and conservation in domestic oil
consumption.

Since the 1983 devaluation Indonesia has introduced a number
of reforms in an effort to broaden and deepen the financial
system and encourage more domestic savings for productive use.
In June 1983 a liberalisation of the banking system transferred greater initiative to commercial banks through the
lifting of credit ceilings and freeing of interest rates. The
former left the Bank of Indonesia without effective monetary
controls, so in January 1984 two new instruments were
announced - discount window facilities and Bank Indonesia
certificates which will allow the central bank to manage the
money supply and influence interest rates through open
market operations.(7)

In January 1984 the government introduced tax reforms aimed
at simplifying the system. Objectives include modernising a
tax system inherited from former colonial times, broadening
the taxpayer base, lowering income tax rates and establishing
a value-added tax as well as a separate sales tax on luxury
goods.(8) A major intention of the reforms is to ensure that

non-oil sector taxes provide a growing share of public sector
revenues to finance development activities planned for
Repelita IV. It is expected the new reforms which substantially broaden the tax base will increase non-oil taxes from
6 per cent of GDP to 10 per cent, and reduce the relative
importance of taxation from the oil and gas sector.

Devaluation, project rescheduling, and monetary and fiscal
reforms in the year following the March 1983 oil price
decreases demonstrate a determined effort by the government
to maintain stability within the economy and induce desired
structural change. A major stumbling block to growth and
efficiency remains the pervasive regulatory system, although
the government has indicated its intention to implement de-
regulation measures as a matter of urgency.(9)

PROBLEMS AND PROSPECTS

'The essence of Indonesia's medium and longer-term
economic problem can be simply stated. The decline
in the world oil price has meant for Indonesia a
sharp deterioration in her terms of trade and capacity
to import. While oil prices may well resume their rise
in the late 1980s, Indonesia's exportable oil sector
surpluses will diminish'.(10)

The above quote from H. W. Arndt very clearly sums up the
major economic problem facing Indonesia. Remedial measures
also become quite clear, i.e. the necessity to reduce imports
and expand non-oil exports. A recent World Bank report
suggests that the current account deficit for 1983/84 was
US$4.2 billion, or about 6 per cent of GNP compared with
US$7.3 billion (8.4 per cent of GNP) in the previous fiscal
year,(11) the main reasons for the reduction being devaluation
and rephasing of large scale projects.

Using the more up to date 1981 price index the World Bank
estimates real growth of GDP at 4.5 per cent in 1983 compared
to zero growth in 1982. Considering the major changes in the
economy, inflation has remained remarkably low - 10 per cent
in 1982 and 12 per cent in 1983.

The World Bank is critical of Repelita IV's forecast annual
current-account deficit of nearly US$5 billion in order to
attain its 5 per cent annual growth target, and feels a
smaller deficit at the expense of a lower overall growth rate
would be more prudent. Foreign loans of about US$4.5 billion

a year to cover the current-account deficit would increase the debt service ratio from an estimated 23 per cent in 1983 to about 28 per cent in 1985, and then gradually decline to about 23 per cent by the end of the decade. However the report insists that Indonesia's overall debt structure remains sound and that projected debt service payments are not excessive judged by international standards.

The Bank's assessment of government policy is somewhat mixed. Whilst labour intensive projects receive greater priority in Repelita IV than the previous five year plan, the government is also spending large amounts on power generation, industry and mining - the most capital-intensive and import-intensive sectors. These sectors may absorb an unduly large share of the limited capital goods available for the public sector, at the expense of other sectors such as agriculture, education, health and regional development.

Indonesia, with comparative advantage in the oil and natural gas sector, but with a burgeoning population, needs to establish a judicious combination of capital-intensive and labour-intensive industries. A growing awareness over recent years that more resources should be directed to the labour-intensive and small industries sector has prompted criticism from both internal and external sources.

The fact that unemployment is a major problem is not disputed, although estimates of its magnitude tend to vary. According to the Ministry of Manpower, an estimated unemployment of 1.5 million in 1983 could reach 4.5 million by the end of Repelita IV in 1989 as approximately two million new entrants to the labour force each year are not fully absorbed. However, if under-employment is translated into an unemployment equivalent, it is thought that 9-10 million people are now unemployed in a total workforce of approximately 60 million, or about 17 per cent unemployed.(12)

In conclusion, the fact that Indonesia has embarked upon a programme of corrective measures indicates a determined effort by the government to maintain economic stability and growth. As with other countries, the government faces the task of attempting to achieve a reasonable balance between economic policies which are not always compatible. Generally it has adopted a pragmatic approach which with certain qualifications has gained the respect of the major international financial institutions, as evidenced by their willingness to maintain supporting loans. Indonesia's immediate fortunes clearly depend on the world oil markets, the future of which would be folly to predict in view of the volatile political situation in some supply areas. However, the recent problems associated with oil prices may be beneficial to Indonesia in the longer run by compelling a more rapid structural change to reduce dependency on oil. Nevertheless, the economic, social and political implications of growing unemployment may prove to be Indonesia's most formidable challenge.

NOTES

(1) According to the National Socio-Economic Survey of 1980 food comprises 69 per cent of average per capita expenditure.
(2) *FEER (Far Eastern Economic Review)* 15 December 1983.
(3) 1974/75 Industrial Census, Biro Pusat Statistek.
(4) *FEER* 22 March 1984.
(5) Figures refer to realised investment. The actual amount of investment realised is much less than approvals. For instance out of US$10.9 billion worth of approvals since 1968, only US$6 billion was realised.
FEER 19 January 1984.
(6) Arndt, H. W.'Study of recent developments', *BIES (Bulletin of Indonesian Economic Studies)*, vol.XIX, no.2, August 1983.
(7) *FEER* 2 February 1984.
(8) *Indonesia Development News,* vol.7, no.6, February 1984.
(9) *FEER* 22 March 1984.
(10) *BIES* August 1983.
(11) *FEER* 17 May 1984, summarising World Bank Report.
(12) *FEER* 8 December 1983.

4 National integration

LESLIE PALMIER

As the national slogan has it, Indonesia is made up of many
in one. But the one is more of a goal than a reality; the
number who can be said to identify themselves with the country
as a whole, and whose interests lie in its integrity and
prosperity, rather than in one or other of its parts, is still
relatively small, and to be found mainly in the large cities,
especially the capital, Jakarta.

But since independence in 1945, and especially since the
transfer of sovereignty in 1949, processes have been at work
making for the creation of an Indonesian society which, while
not denying its roots in local cultures, will nevertheless
have a recognisable integrity. And I believe it is fair to
say that even those Indonesians still restricted to their
local cultures see this emerging society as the goal of the
future; if not of themselves, then of their children and
grandchildren.

To a very great degree, the development of the new Indonesia
is synonymous with the modernisation of the society. As
Indonesians see it, this involves acquiring and applying
Western knowledge in such a way as not only to permit, but
also to encourage and strengthen, their own cultures. Needless to say, there are considerable difficulties in achieving
this objective; the incompatibilities are evident enough.
Also, there are only individual ethnic cultures; there is no

traditional national culture. This is in process of being
created at the moment as Indonesians of various origins mix
and treat with one another and evolve a common language of
symbols.

If there is one word that will summarise the processes
making for this new Indonesian society it is 'communication':
the development of links, by means of both human and physical,
between Indonesians of various origins. One of the most
important is, of course, education, and the progress achieved
here is quite remarkable.

The Netherlands Indies of pre-war, in pursuit of its policy
of maintaining native cultures, provided schooling that was
both divided and stratified. There were several varieties of
primary and secondary education, oriented to the European,
Chinese, and Native population groups. (Furnivall 1944, p.337)
It was also severely limited; according to the 1930 Census,
only 6 per cent of the population were literate in any
language.

The present-day structure of education was established by
the Japanese during their occupation of the country. They
abolished all the various divisions within primary and secondary education, and set up one system of lower education,
consisting of six years of elementary school, three years of
secondary, and three years of high school. Most important,
Indonesian replaced Dutch as the medium of instruction in all
schools, not merely those intended for the village population.
(Dep. P. & K. 1979, p.88-9) To all intents and purposes, this
structure still obtains today within the state sector. There
are in addition several private (including mission) schools.
It is worth remarking that educational expansion is the one
programme which has prospered despite the country's political
vicissitudes, mentioned in the Introduction. There appears
to have been a consensus among Indonesians of all origins
and shades of opinion that what they needed was education, as
much and as rapidly as possible. The figures indicate the
growth that has been achieved. In 1950 the number of
elementary school pupils numbered some 5 million. (Dep. P. &
K. 1979, p.101) By the time of the 1980 census, there were
nearly 21 million children between the ages of 7 and 12 at
primary school. (CBS 1981, p.28) This very much more than
compensates for the growth in the population from 81 million
in 1954 to, say, 160 million in 1980. If we consider the
proportion of the age group which was enrolled, whereas only
6 per cent attended secondary school in 1960, by 1975 the
figure was 33 per cent. (CBS 1978, p.126) As a result both of

the regular educational programmes, and also mass education, illiteracy has been greatly reduced. In 1930, 94 per cent were illiterate, as mentioned above. The 1980 census found that this figure had been reduced to 32 per cent.

In the nature of the case, however, primary and secondary education remain still rather local, if only because pupils are likely to participate in the same culture. The better indicator of unification is perhaps higher education. This does not, of course, indicate in every case participation in a national culture; the truly Indonesian universities, that is those drawing students from anywhere in the archipelago, are only some half dozen or so. But the catchment area even for most of the others is still larger than any one ethnic culture. So the figures for enrolment in higher education deserve attention.

The first university institution was the Technical College set up in Bandung in 1920; its lineal descendant is the very prestigious Institute of Technology at Bandung, known as ITB. It was followed by Colleges of Law, Medicine, and Literature and Philosophy, an Academy for Civil Servants at Jakarta, a School of Dental Surgery in Surabaya, and a College of Agriculture in Bogor. The Dutch attempted throughout to maintain standards on a par with institutions in Europe, but the specialists produced were very few. The number of professionally trained Indonesians in 1942 was estimated at little more than a thousand: 400 engineers; 400 physicians; 250 lawyers, several veterinarians and agriculturists, and a few in other disciplines. (HRAF 1956, II, p.402)

Since independence, development has been rapid, both in the state sector and the private. In the latter the number enrolled in recent years has surpassed those in the state. It remains true, however, that the state universities are those with the higher standards, and the most sought after. Their degrees are of course automatically accepted as job qualifications by the state, which is the largest employer. However, degrees from the private universities are given equal standing provided the awarding institution (whether a university, a faculty, or even a department within a faculty) has obtained official recognition. Otherwise, private university graduates may still obtain recognised degrees by taking examinations set and assessed by state university teachers.

The degrees awarded by the higher education institutions are principally of two kinds: the Bachelor, called *Sarjana Muda*, and the Master, or *Sarjana*. The latter is considered the true university degree, indicating as its name implies a mastery of the subject studied. The Bachelor is used more as the terminal qualification of Academies, which provide vocational training of one kind or another.

To take the Master degrees first. In 1950, a mere 73 were awarded and these all came from the State universities. By 1979 the State Universities and the Teacher Training Institutes (created in the 1960s) had together awarded 9,300, mostly the universities. The state institutions had awarded even more Bachelor degrees; rising from (in round figures) 10,300 in 1974 (the first year for which there are centralised records) to 14,300 in 1979. To these one must add the private state-recognised graduates. There were 5,600 Bachelors in 1976; they had risen to 10,2000 in 1980. Masters were 7,000 in 1976; by 1980 they were 12,000. The table below gives the exact figures

Table 4.1
Graduates

Year	State Universities and Teacher-training Institutes		State-recognised Private Institutions	
	Master	Bachelor	Master	Bachelor
1950	73			
1974	6,132	10,303		
1976	7,102	13,697	1,504	5,586
1978	8,595	13,509		
1980			1,909	10,228

Sources: Lembaga Ilmu Pengetahuan Indonesia, Jakarta, *Jumlah Sarjana Lulusan dari 40 Perguruan Tinggi Negeri di Indonesia, 1950-1973*, Jakarta, 1974; Departement Pendidikan dan Kebudayaan, Direktorat Jenderal Pendidikan Tinggi, *Data Perguruan Tinggi Negeri 1974-78*, Jakarta, 1980; *Ibid.*, Direktorat Perguruan Tinggi Swasta, *Data dan Informasi Tentang Perguruan Tinggi Swasta Sampai Tahun 1980*, Jakarta, n.d.

As a natural consequence, the number of graduates in the population has grown rapidly. The table below shows that the graduates of both combined in the total population, amounting to only 55,800 in 1961, had grown nearly tenfold, to 545,300 twenty years later.

Table 4.2
Graduates in Total Population 10 Years of Age and Over

Consus Year	Total	Bachelor	Master etc.
1961	55,837	34,850	21,257
1971	200,294	99,343	100,951
1980	545,257	315,629	229,628

This rapid expansion of the graduate population has not been achieved without the cost of a lowering of standards below the pre-war level. But the decision was taken early in Indonesia's independent history that quality had to be sacrificed for quantity; better to have large numbers with a little literacy, a little schooling, than a few with degrees of international standard and a vast mass of illiterates.

The policy of expansion, particularly in the islands other than Java, is still being followed, but since 1974 it has been allied to a serious attempt to raise the level of both the state and the private sectors. Standards, however, are still low, and it is not uncommon for children of senior officials and other rich parents to be sent abroad for their higher education.

In creating a national consciousness, a crucial role is played by women, since it is they who have in their hands the early training of children. There is no underestimation of their role in Indonesia; as elsewhere in South East Asia, women traditionally have enjoyed far higher position than in either India or China or, until fairly recently, in Europe. However, it would seem that they are not participating fully in the process of education. Thus, the figures for school attendance obtained for the 1980 Census show that 36 per cent of women had never or not yet attended school, against only 24 per cent of men; while there were 24 per cent women attending, against 28 per cent men. Similarly, with regard to illiteracy, while both men and women have made progress, the men have done so more. In 1930, there was 98 per cent female illiteracy, against 89 per cent male; in 1980, it was 36 per cent female, against only 19 per cent male.

The female disadvantage in education would not appear to be due to any lack of receptivity to modern ideas. To take a matter at once most intimate and most likely to elicit instinctive rejection, birth control. In the early days of the programme, in 1971/72, less than 3 per cent of married women were recorded as users of family planning methods. (CBS 1978, p.38) This was a figure produced by the National Family

70

Planning Board, so was not likely to be an underestimate. The census of 1980 showed that the figure had risen to 27 per cent. Interestingly, there was very little difference, less than one percentage point, between the rural and urban proportions. It is clear, then, that adult women have little reluctance to accept modern values; the reason for their being given less than their fair share of education is probably to be traced to the attitudes more of the parents than of the girls themselves.

Turning to the physical communications, we have some figures for the increase in motor vehicles, reproduced in Table 4.3. Not surprisingly, perhaps, the greatest growth has been in motor-cycles, which are both economical and suited to the Indonesian climate. Public vehicles, buses and lorries, have increased more rapidly than motor cars.

Table 4.3
Registered Motor Vehicles

	1971		1978	
	No.	Per 10,000 Population	No.	Per 10,000 Population
Cars	259,282	21.58	535,552	37.83
Lorries	115,082	9.58	335,699	23.71
Buses	22,797	1.90	58,583	4.14
Motor-cycles	528,079	43.95	1,983,322	140.08

Sources: CBS 1978, p.87; 1979, p.111.

As a further indicator one may consider the spread of telephones. As Table 4.4 shows, they have increased from 18 per 10,000 in 1971, to 32 per 10,000 in 1978.

Table 4.4
Number of Telephones and Ratio per 10,000 Population

	Number	Ratio
1971	221,780	18.46
1974	284,481	22.07
1978	447,031	31.57

Sources: *Ibid.*

One of the most powerful means of communication is, of course, the mass media. In the last couple of decades Indonesia has seen emerge a proliferation of newspapers and magazines. This should not be taken as a sign of freedom of expression, a point elaborated later. For all practical purposes, statements of political opinion are not permitted, unless they are in accordance with state policy already decided. Nevertheless, there is little doubt that the mass media are exhibiting models of behaviour for the new Indonesians. In the nature of the case, since many of the situations faced by   Indonesians have no precedent in indigenous culture, the models offered as example are often foreign, particularly Western.

Consumption of the printed mass media, however, requires literacy and a minimum level of income. This does not apply to the same extent to radio, which is cheaper than either newspapers or television. The 1978 national socio-economic survey found that 50 per cent of the population aged ten plus listened to the radio, against only 20 per cent who looked at television, and 17 per cent who read newspapres. (CBS 1981, p.40) This was an advance on 1976, when 40 per cent listened to the radio, 6 per cent looked at television, while 7 per cent read newspapers. (CBS 1976, p.28)

Whilst the growth in the number who are exposed to the mass media is impressive, it should not be exaggerated. In 1976 it was found that 70 per cent of households had no access to any of these media. Even in the urban areas, 40 per cent of households were so deprived. (CBS 1976, pp.25-6) It should, too, be mentioned that the greatest output of radio, both state and private, is entertainment, particularly pop music. Television, which is a state monopoly, offers somewhat more serious material, cultural and educational programmes being given importance. In both media, however, news is a government preserve, and independent reports or commentaries are not permitted. Foreign news is relatively uncensored, apart from the omission or toning down of reports critical of the government's policy.

The mass media cannot therefore be said to be presenting Indonesians with an accurate picture of the world. Their value perhaps lies more in accustoming him to a common national output to which he can relate. Certainly considerable effort goes into showing Indonesians who have access to television (mostly the better-off) the ways of life of their compatriots in other provinces.

Education, communications, the mass media, are, of course, most concentrated in the urban areas. It is here, to repeat myself, that the Indonesian is being created. The growth of urbanisation in Indonesia has been impressive. If we take cities with a population of more than 100,000, their aggregate population at the time of the 1930 census was under 3 million, when the population was 61 million. By 1971 the total population had grown to 120 million, of whom 14 million were in the cities; (CBS 1978, pp.24-5) in other words a rise from one twentieth to one ninth. The pace has continued since. In 1971, 17 per cent of the population was living in urban areas (i.e. 25,000 and above); (*Ibid.*, p.22) the 1980 census gave a figure of 22 per cent.

These various means of knitting the country into a single allegiance are of considerable importance, when one remembers that the divisions within the country, whether represented by political party or religion, sometimes emerging into revolt, often had a very substantial regional, not to say ethnic, base. So the process of government in Indonesia, from the declaration of its independence in 1945, has fundamentally consisted of an attempt to substitute national loyalties for local ones. The advent of the New Order marked a further attempt towards national integration.

The regime came in imbued with a firmly-held belief in its right to rule, formally expressed in the philosophy of the Dual Function, or *Dwi-Fungsi*, to the effect that the military have the task not only of defending the state from internal and external attack, but also of playing their full part in its governance. This is buttressed by the ideology, produced by military officers with little prompting, that Indonesia's existence is primarily due to their efforts. They argue that at the time of the second Dutch attack on the infant republic they alone refused to surrender; Sukarno and the other civilian leaders, instead of taking to the jungle, allowed themselves to be led into captivity. The theory conveniently overlooks the fact that the military encounters with the Dutch were, at best, indecisive; it was, as noted in the Introduction above and by Dr. Leifer below, the Indonesian civilian leaders' skill in courting world opinion and playing off the Americans against the Russians that gave Indonesia its sovereignty. Nevertheless, this is little acknowledged now, at least publicly.

From the start, the New Order set economic development as its goal, with a policy not dissimilar to the Japanese Meiji leaders' slogan of 1870: 'Rich country, strong army'. And the

goal was to be attained, it soon became clear, in military
fashion. The whole country was to march, in uniform style,
with no questioning of orders or criticism of superior
officers. Conformity was to be the watch-word.

The first system to be reformed was the political. The
regime reasoned that many of the country's disruptions, within
the state as outside it, could be traced to the activities
of one or other political party which, as already mentioned,
was often linked with an ethnic group. So what was sought
was a depoliticised form of government. In theory at least,
this did not mean the end of representation. The notion was
that democratic institutions had been launched on the
Indonesian people before they were ready for them. So the
institutions decreed by the 1945 Constitution, in force when
the New Order was inaugurated, were to be maintained, but they
were to be protected from undue strain. That Constitution
prescribes a Presidential cabinet. The cabinet is responsible not to parliament, but to the President, and he is
responsible only to the Popular Consultative Assembly
(*Majelis Permusjarawatan Rakyat*), which meets once every
four years. Half of the members of this Assembly are made
up of the Parliament, or *Dewan Parwakilan Rakyat*. The New
Order sought to ensure that both assemblies would be sup-
portive, not critical. In passing, it might be mentioned
that Indonesians generally regard the adversary system which
is enshrined in our own unwritten constitution, from parliament to the law courts, as socially damaging. So the regime
had plenty of support, as had had the late President Sukarno
in his day, in these aims. The first steps it took to
achieving them were concerned with political parties. In
Indonesia politicians are not considered necessarily representatives of the people, but rather specialists in the
political art. Therefore, there was considerable backing
for the previous President Sukarno's notion of a Functional
Grouping, which would represent people by their employment,
rather than by the political parties they supported, an idea
perhaps drawn from theories of the corporate state. The
regime gave considerably greater importance to this functional
grouping which it developed into a political party called
Golkar, whose function is to support the Government, from
whom in turn it obtains considerable backing and material
resources.

The political parties proper were also operated upon. First,
they were assembled into two groupings, Muslim and non-Muslim,
the first called 'developmental', the second ' democratic',
in which individual parties rapidly lost their identity.

This, however, was not enough. Using various means of pressure, those leaders not amenable to the regime were soon replaced by more plastic individuals.

Not only were the political parties emasculated and shrunk, but also they were deprived of most of their constituencies. The 'intellectuals' of the regime produced a theory of the 'floating mass', which should not be confused with the 'floating vote' dear to British psephologists. The 'floating mass' refers to villagers. The theory held that they were unnecessarily confused by the agitation of political parties when they should be getting on with their work. So political parties were banned from all canvassing in the villages except at election times; in between the villagers were to be concerned with development.

The effect of these changes is evident enough. There is now no official political opposition, formal or informal. Members of these assemblies are not expected to challenge government policy but only, at best, to suggest improvements to legislation or, occasionally, to bring to light instances where the legislation is being flouted. For the most part, however, they are an obedient claque.

Also to be operated upon were the government departments. When the New Order came to power, they were grazing grounds fought over by the political parties. Loyalty to the party counted for much more than efficiency or honesty. As a natural consequence, incompetence and corruption were widespread, and no government could be sure that its instructions would be carried out, particularly if senior positions in a department were held by men in opposition political parties.

The New Order attempted to remedy this by ensuring that of the three leading figures in a government department, at least one was a military man. It could thus ensure that the instructions of the government were carried out. Needless to say, this went along with, at the beginning of the New Order, purges of the disloyal and doubtful. Furthermore, a system of payments was established for officials which can be manipulated to ensure loyalty; this meaning, of course, the absence of criticism of decisions taken by superiors. Recent statements indicate satisfaction with the present state of affairs in the departments. There is no dangerous corruption, we are told, meaning corruption linked to disloyalty to the state. Corruption not so connected is regarded as a venial failing.

The rural areas were already, under Sukarno's Guided
Democracy, largely under military control. A military counterpart sat alongside the civilian administrator at all levels,
down to the sergeant in the village. The New Order streng-
thened the military hold, with many senior officers being
appointed governors of provinces.

There remained only two sources of criticism, the mass media
and the students. The radio had always been under government control; television, as it developed, followed the same
line. The press, however, had been free at least at independence and until the inception of 'Guided Democracy' in
1959. It regained much of its freedom with the coming of the
New Order, which it saw as a liberation. However, when the
new rulers found themselves being criticised they rapidly
took action to muzzle the newspapers. It now requires only
a mild criticism of either government policy or personalities
for a newspaper to find its printing or its publishing
licence revoked and thus itself suspended. Sometimes, this
is terminal, as in the case of two of the best newspapers
Indonesia has produced, namely *Pedoman* and *Indonesia Raya*.
More often, perhaps, the suspension is for a length of time
to cause financial injury. In other words, the regime is
happy for the newspapers to purvey authorised accounts of
events, but not to criticise government. This, however, is
not enough. A newspaper may find itself warned, and even
suspended, if it gives a perfectly factual account of events
within the country which the regime would prefer not known.

With the politicians, officials, and mass media, under
control, there remained only one source of possible dissent,
that is the students in the universities. It is from these
groupings that emerged agitation against the corrupt wealth
of the few at the top of Indonesian society, against the form
of development followed, which at the time certainly favoured
the urban areas, particularly the capital city, and somewhat
neglected the rural. (It is important to mention that since
then the regime has gone some way to correct the imbalance, as
Mr. Walton shows below.)

So radical measures were taken to put an end to the frequent
student expressions of discontent. This was done, in essence,
by first disbanding the autonomous student councils, and then
recreating them in a new form, where they were chaired by
the Rector (or academic head) of the university, who was
made specifically responsible for discipline on his campus.
This has certainly had the effect desired by the regime; one
does not now hear of student protests of any kind.

So, in brief, all independent and critical voices have been silenced. Even those few retired senior generals, who thought that their services to the Army and the country permitted them to criticise abuses, have been speedily disillusioned by the threat of withdrawal of their retirement privileges. Though the brutality of the first few years of the New Order, when large numbers of suspected Communists were sent to penal colonies, has not been repeated, the methods followed have been effective.

Meanwhile, the forms of constitutional democracy are maintained. The domesticated political groupings are permitted to canvass for votes at election times in competition with one another and with *Golkar*. As it enjoys government support, predictably, it garners the mass of votes; the only question from one election to another is whether the Muslim grouping achieves a higher or lower total than in the previous election. It is of interest that foreign correspondents are not permitted to visit the rural areas at election times; the reasons are perhaps obvious.

The voting figures are solemnly used to justify the continuance of the regime and its policies. It is a fascinating question, yet to be explored, why so much store is set upon following the forms of democracy, a charade which deceives nobody, neither at home nor abroad. A charitable interpretation would be that the regime still believes that the people are not yet capable of making wise choices of representatives, and so must be given experience of the forms first, before they are allowed to affect the content. But this has slipped, it must be suspected, into a self-justifying system, which ensures that there is no challenge to those already in power. It might be called a mild form of the 'Democratic Centralism' of Leninist theory.

Given the few outlets for the expression of discontent, it is perhaps natural that Islam has become its focus. It is necessary here to speak carefully to avoid exaggeration. For census purposes, some 90 per cent of the population are classed as Muslims. But if one asks the largest single ethnic group, namely the Javanese, most of these will acknowledge that they are '*Islam statistik*', that is to say Muslims for statistical purposes only. (There may here be a parallel with the number in this country identified as Church of England.) Genuine commitment to Islam is perhaps to be found more frequently in the areas which were not too deeply imbued with previous Hindu and Buddhist or Christian influences. These areas are, especially, parts of Sumatra,

West Java, Kalimantan (Borneo), and South Sulawesi (Celebes).
It has been noteworthy that leaders of Muslim dissident groups
put on trial in recent years have usually not been Javanese.

Also, though there has been a considerable increase in the
number of Indonesians actively practising their Islam, by no
means all of them are opposed to the regime; many are only
too well aware of the benefits they derive from it. The point
at issue is the constitution of the state. The political
Muslims' maximum demand is that Islamic Law be in force for
all; their minimum that it be applied to all Muslims. The
non-political Muslims refuse both. They accept the principle
of a secular state, whilst providing lavish support for
religion. One important reason for their stand is that they
fear that the non-Islamic areas of Indonesia, such as Bali
and North Celebes, might well be tempted to secede rather
than accept Islamic Law. Another reason may also perhaps
be ventured. It is that they are well aware that the reason
for the backwardness of the Middle East is precisely the
application of Islamic Law, and modern governments there go
to some very strange shifts in order not to apply Islamic
Law while maintaining it. In one phrase, they fear that
Islamic Law would prevent the necessary adaptation not only
of the society, but of Islam itself, to the exigencies of
the modern world.

Of the support by the government for Islam there is little
question. Since independence one government department, that
of Religion, has been dominated by Islamic teachers, with
the task of subsidising them throughout the country. Funds
are provided for Islamic education, for the building of
mosques, for the pilgrimage to Mecca. If one takes this last
alone, those making the pilgrimage have grown from 55,000 in
1975-76, partly by sea and partly by air, to 73,000 in 1978-
79, all by air.

It is therefore probably unnecessary to say that no easy
parallels should be drawn with Iran under the late Shah.
He had completely alienated the Islamic clergy in his country
and, in many cases, deprived them of important sources of
income. All governments of Indonesia have done exactly the
reverse, and have so far successfully incorporated the Islamic
teachers into the structure of the state; it is worth
remarking that a number of prominent generals obtained part
or all of their education in Islamic day schools *(madrassah)*
and boarding schools *(pesantren)*. While Islam will therefore
continue to act as a focus for the discontented, it is doubtful if the Muslim leadership will espouse their causes.

However, it is also true that, in principle at least, the zealous Muslim is expected to work for an Islamic state. He certainly owes no allegiance to an unbeliever state, which happily is not the case for Indonesia. The Muslims in government, beginning with the President, make a point of public devotions. Nevertheless, the fact that Indonesia is not an Islamic state remains a constant irritant to the political Muslims. It is round the symbol of Islam that the resentments tend to coalesce, and have issued, for example, in attacks on the homes of the rich. For these purposes the rich are usually defined as those of Chinese descent. The fact that there are now many Indonesians richer than very many Chinese somehow does not attract the ire of the mobs. It may be, of course, that these are not *kaffir* (unbelievers); it also may be that many of them are either military officers or connected with the military, and the ringleaders of the mobs fear reprisals. The Chinese have no such protection.

This is not to imply that the Chinese are the objects of the regime's animosity. If anything, the reverse is the case; some of their richest entrepreneurs are in close concert with prominent figures in the New Order. As a group, the Chinese have undoubtedly benefited considerably from the measures of economic development taken by the government. It has also attempted to protect them from being the perennial object of mob hatred by forcibly, in military fashion, assimilating them into the majority culture. Chinese were encouraged to adopt Indonesian names, though since both names are known and used together in, for example, news reports and obituaries, it is not clear what has been achieved by that measure. Also, the use of Chinese characters is forbidden, even in imported printed matter,(1) and all Chinese schools have been abolished. All this forced homogeneity does not so far seem to make much difference to the dislike in which the Chinese are held, as the riots mentioned indicate.

How well has this system worked? Economically, as the papers by both Harvey Demaine and John Walton have shown, creditably enough. Indonesia has at least kept up with the other South East Asian economies; compared with its own performance between 1950 and 1966, it has done extremely well. No doubt, one reason for this is that governmental stability, however achieved, was bound to result in economic progress. At the same time, however, it is arguable that the system adopted, where those with power are unquestioned, has led to great waste. The most dramatic example, perhaps, was the management of the State Oil Concern, Pertamina, by General Sutowo, a former Army physician of unquestioned entrepre-

neurial talents. Backed by powerful figures, including the
President, he was quite out of the control of his formal
superior, the Minister of Mines, and openly permitted his
subordinates to amass fortunes through corruption. His own
dubious financial procedures, as Dr. Demaine has mentioned,
cost the Indonesian state a very large sum of money, and
without doubt set back its development. A system more open
to criticism might well have prevented such a catastrophe, by
bringing Dr. Sutowo to account much earlier. But this is
only one example. The report of the Commission of Four
elder statesmen a decade ago showed that waste and corruption
were commonplace. While some measures have been taken to
control junior officials, the senior remain unassailable.

There is also little doubt that the refusal to allow those
in authority, at all levels, to be criticised by their subordinates has contributed to the great widening in income
levels which has taken place. It may well be true that the
mass of Indonesians, with some exceptions, are better off
than they were; what is undeniable is that a very small
percentage of the population are living in very great luxury,
often attained by dubious means, which their position does
not permit to be criticised. This has been a cause of great
resentment, both by the middle classes on fixed salaries,
and by the poor. Of this the government is well aware, to
the extent that even a relatively unimportant riot, which
elsewhere would be dealt with quite adequately by normal
policing, calls for the blanketing of the area by troops,
the blacking out of news about the incident in the newspapers,
and no mention of it on the radio, even to the cutting of
telephone links for a while.

However, the result of silencing all sources of criticism
has been that the government now has within the country no
reliable measure of its own performance in either the political or economic sphere. Its own officials, including those in
the intelligence bodies, know only too well the penalties of
conveying bad news to their superiors, who in turn are aware
of the unreliability of the information they are fed. And
no newspaper dare print material which could be construed as
a criticism of the regime or its policies. From this comes,
of course, the very great importance given by the government
itself to such external agencies as the World Bank and the
surveys it conducts and finances, which thereby acquire a
certain protection. It is worth noting that the changes in
development policy have usually followed suggestions from
the World Bank and other international agencies.

It used at one time to be thought that economic development was the way to relieve poverty and so discontent (and, thereby, of course, keep out the Communists). Experience has shown this belief to be ill-founded. Development of its nature entails much upheaval, the abandonment of traditional ways and values, giving rise to great stress, as we in Britain do not need to be reminded. In addition, in a case such as Indonesia, it means the very rapid expansion of education, often on foreign models which imply an egalitarian structure of discussion. In particular, the many thousands of specialists being produced by the tertiary institutions and congregated in the cities are not to be equated with the simple peasants from whom they sprang, who would have been well prepared to accept without question the instructions of their betters. It must be doubted if the best policy for the new society is to stifle all ventilation of critical opinion; the innovativeness required for the country's development will not be encouraged thereby, and to drive all discontent underground and so render government ignorant of social movements, seems to be laying trouble in store.

NOTE

(1) A magazine photograph of the interior of, say, a Hong Kong hotel will be distributed in Indonesia with any Chinese characters obliterated by sticky black ink.

BIBLIOGRAPHY

CBS, Indonesia, Central Bureau of Statistics, *Indonesian Social Developmental Atlas, 1930-1978*, Jakarta, 1978.
CBS, *Ibid., Social Indicators, 1978*, Jakarta, 1979.
CBS, *Ibid.,Keadaan Sosial-Budaya Penduduk, 1976*, Jakarta, 1976.
CBS, *Ibid., Socio-Cultural Conditions of the Population, 1978*, Jakarta, 1981.
Dep. P. & K., Departemen Pendidikan dan Kebudayaan, *Dari Jaman Ke Jaman*, Jakarta, 1979.

Furnivall, J. S. *Netherlands India*, Cambridge, 1944.
HRAF, Human Relations Area Files, New Haven, Conn. USA, *Area Handbook on Indonesia*, 3 vols, New Haven, 1956.

5 Drama and society

ANGELA HOBART

Indonesia has a rich and complex artistic tradition. Theatre
is perhaps the most developed art form, with the highest
repute, and which appeals to the greatest number of people.
In the West theatre has become increasingly a luxury which
mainly the educated urban elite indulge in after work; it is
for them a pleasurable way of passing time.   In contrast,
theatre in Indonesia, as in most of South East Asia, is an
integral part of the culture, expressing through patterns of
forms, colours, movements and sounds a fund of values which
are widely shared. These relate to the political, religious,
moral and aesthetic life of the society as a whole or of a
particular group.

In what follows, attention is focused on Java and Bali as
they have maintained the most vigorous and venerated dramatic
activities in Indonesia. Java is the most populous island,
containing over eighty million people, with a complex historical and cultural background. The people of central and
east Java, together with the Balinese, have also reached a
high degree of civilisation, which those from other parts of
the archipelago, including the Sudanese of west Java, have not
yet attained.

There is a tremendous variety of theatre genres on the two
islands including the shadow play, puppet shows, the masked
dance, operetta, and pure dance forms. The beginning of

theatre can be traced back to prehistoric times. However, the foundations of the later development of the classical theatre, especially the shadow play and dance drama, were laid when Indian culture diffused over the islands from about 200 AD to 1,000 AD.

In this paper I want to look at two theatre forms - the shadow play and contemporary drama. The former is the most revered because of its religious significance. I will then discuss the popular proletarian drama, *ludruk*, in Java and its equivalent form in Bali. A comparative study of these genres of theatre is facilitated by the fact that there are excellent works on these in Java, and I have myself studied them in Bali (1970-72 and 1980). As the subject is so extensive, I will make only a few relevant comments on these different forms of theatre.

JAVA

The shadow play (*wayang kulit*) and proletarian drama (*ludruk*)

The classic form of the shadow play belongs to the Great Tradition which evolved to its greatest efflorescence in Java at the courts of Surakarta and Jogjakarta during the last three centuries. The values it expresses are largely those of the *priyayi*, the hereditary aristocracy who, since the time of the Dutch, belong to the white-collar élite and are often found in the civil service (Geertz 1966, p.288). These values have nevertheless penetrated throughout the culture and are fairly generally respected by the people (Anderson 1965, p.5).

The shadow play is so called because the puppets, which are flat cut-outs of leather, carefully painted and chiselled, with rods as handles, are used to project shadows on to a screen. They are manipulated by a story-teller or puppeteer (*dalang*), in accompaniment to percussion music in the background. He is also a ritual practitioner who recites religious incantations before and after the performance.

Most stories dramatised are drawn from the great Hindu epics, the *Ramayana* and the *Mahabharata*. As the latter epic tends to be more frequently performed than the former, I shall primarily focus on it here. The *Mahabharata* is concerned with the conflict between two families, the five semi-divine Pandawa brothers and their first cousins, the 100 Korawa brothers. The crucial question to be settled is who are the rightful heirs to the throne of Nastina. The tensions between the cousins culminates in the great war, the *Bharatayuddha*, which

lasts for eighteen horrendous days. Finally the Korawas are
defeated and the eldest Pandawa brother, Yudistira, comes to
the throne. Throughout the Pandawas are guided by Krishna,
their mentor.

The puppets represent from 100 to 300 characters who can be
classified into three main types: the nobles, the servants and
the ogres. The majority of nobles fall into two groups, the
Pandawas and Korawas, with their respective followers. The
Pandawas tend to be characterised by their elegant looks; most
have refined almond-shaped eyes and graceful bodies. The
Korawas, on the other hand, are built on a larger scale and
have big, round eyes, indicative of coarseness and lack of
control. The ogres have sturdy, muscular bodies, wild hair
and coarse features. Unlike the other characters, who are
derived from the epic literature, the servants or clowns are
probably pre-Hindu in origin. They are coarse and distorted
in appearance.

It is primarily between the eighteenth and twentieth centuries
that the shadow play developed under court patronage into such
a sophisticated and complex theatre genre. Puppeteers were
retainers of the court, and were supported by the sultan. The
performances were generally given, as is still the case, in
grand ceremonies of rites-of-passage. There was no entrance
fee, and the sultan invited selected guests to attend. It was
during this time that other art forms flourished, the main
ones being the patterns of the wax-dyed textiles, *batik*, and
the structure of the percussion orchestra, *gamelan*. The rules
of etiquette and language to mark status and rank became
increasingly elaborate. It is, though, above all the shadow
play which was valued for the philosophical and mystical
insights it provided for the spectators. This comes vividly
to the fore in the late Sultan Mangkunagara VII of Surakarta's
(1895-1944) paper on the shadow play, where he points out that
his aim is 'to dare to lift a small tip of the veil to show
how in *wayang* (the shadow play) performance, lies hidden the
secret knowledge concerning the deepest significance of life'
(1957, p.1).

In order to understand something of the significance that the
shadow play has for the élite, it is important to realise that
the stage and the equipment used by the puppeteer is symbolic
and suggests a higher order of reality. In the mystico-
religious literature of the nineteenth century this is
summarised as follows:

   'The illuminated screen is the visible world. The puppets,
   which are arranged in an orderly fashion at the beginning

84

of the play, are the different varieties and categories
created by God. The banana trunk into which the *dalang*
sticks the puppets is the surface of the earth.

The lamp over the head of the *dalang*, which brings life to
the shadows, is the lamp of life. The motives and
melodies of the *gamelan* orchestra, fixed in accordance with
the various persons and events projected on the screen,
represent the harmony and mutual relationship of everything which exists in the world.

He who refuses to be led by one who is wiser than he, or a
guru (i.e. the *dalang*, who is likened to God), will never
gain the right knowledge of all that exists and will go
astray.'

(Adapted from Zoetmulder 1971, p.89.)

In other words, Truth is veiled and cannot be easily grasped.
It can, though, be glimpsed by members of the élite, with the
help of a teacher (implying in this case the puppeteer),
during a play on the stage which is a replica of the macrocosm.
It is with this cosmological framework in mind that I want to
discuss the significance of the shadow theatre.

Within the cosmological setting symbolised by the stage, the
Pandawas and Korawas are linked to the system of complementary
opposites found in both Java and Bali: right/left; young/old;
male/female; refinement/coarseness; virtue/baseness and so
forth. In this theory the relative baseness of the Korawas is
necessary to offset and complement the relative virtue of the
Pandawas. Their balance is intrinsic to world order.

In order for there to be harmony in the *wayang* world, conflict must first occur in a play; this resolves itself in
victory for the semi-divine Pandawas. So cosmic equilibrium
is re-established, for virtue must repeatedly reassert itself;
it cannot exist without its opposite. Arjuna, the third
Pandawa brother, is the prince who epitomises the truly
refined, or *alus*, hero. His appearance is elegant, his conduct dignified and he shows constant awareness of the correct
forms of etiquette, which primarily implies the avoidance of
any act suggestive of disorder or lack of self-discipline.
These qualities contrast with those of the Korawas or the
ogres, who are *kasar*, meaning rough, uncivilised, proud,
clumsy and uncontrolled.

In the society it was above all the king and later the
sultan and his dignitaries, and nowadays the *priyayi*, who

sought to emulate the refined qualities associated with the
Pandawas in theatre. In the early Hindu-Javanese kingdoms,
from the eighth to the thirteenth centuries, the king was the
apex of society, which was highly stratified. He was considered a God incarnate who possessed the mystic light of royalty
(Schrieke 1956, p.83 ff.). Like the emperor of ancient China
(Weber 1951, pp.30-2), the king was the highest spiritual
authority who was responsible for harmony in the cosmos and
his palace was conceived of as the centre of the universe.
Through his inner tranquillity, poise, and nobility, he was
able to mediate between the celestial and mundane worlds, and
prevent calamities from occurring. Even after the collapse of
the Hindu kingdom of Majapahit in the fourteenth century these
notions of kingship were reinstituted through Mataram, the
nominally Islamised sultanate which reached its zenith during
the regime of Sultan Agung from 1613 to 1645. These ideas,
moreover, continued to permeate Javanese society after the
defeat of Mataram by the Dutch, up to the present day.
Although Islam did not permit man to be God incarnate, the
sultan was still considered representative of the god. Hence
all the titles of the sultans of Surakarta perpetuated the anc
ancient concept of the ruler's duty to maintain order in the
cosmos from his palace, which was a microcosm of the macrocosm.
In accordance with this, they bear the title Paku Buwana, Spike
(or Axis) of the World (Holt 1967, p.152). Later rulers
emphasised their divine right to rule by direct identification
with one of the Pandawas. For example, President Sukarno
referred to himself as Gatotkaca, the son of Bima, the
tempestuous, powerful second Pandawa brother, whose father was
a god of wind, Bayu. Sukarno further associated the five
principles of the Indonesian state, the *pancasila* - Faith in
God, Nationalism, Humanism, Democracy and Social Justice - with
the five Pandawa brothers (Holt 1967, pp. 124, 202). It is
also worth noting that the Indonesian Communist Party (PKI)
utilised Arjuna, the third Pandawa brother, identifying his
magical arrow, Pasopati, with the hammer and sickle insignia.
Moreover, before the abortive coup of 1965, both the Nationalist Party (PNI) and the Communists sought to identify themselves with the Pandawas and their opponents with the Korawas.
It is of interest in this context that the present President
Suharto refers to himself as Rama, the noble prince of the
Ramayana, who rescues his wife Sita from the clutches of the
demon king, Rawana.

However, the court shadow play has an additional meaning for
the individual member of the élite, which is not accessible to
the common man or to the uninitiated, and which requires a
teacher, or *guru*. A play encourages the spiritual exercise of

semadi, by which knowledge is obtained of one's divine origin in order to become one with the Absolute. Although the shadow theatre adapts with equal ease to both Javanese and Islamic mysticism (Zoetmulder 1971, pp.85-96), the goal of *semadi* points to India where various salvation doctrines were elaborated by the élite to escape from the mundane world (Weber 1958, pp.166-80). The best-known story dramatised in the shadow theatre which illuminates this goal is called *Bima Suci* (Bima Purified) which is still performed for special occasions. In this story Bima seeks the waters of immortality which Mangkunagara VII interpreted as 'the way to oneness, or to the knowledge of origin and destination' (1957, p.16). After overcoming numerous obstacles, Bima destroys a serpent who threatens him, so symbolically severing the last bond with temporal existence. He then enters into the depth of the ocean which in Javanese mystical literature is described as 'the world filled with light and no shadows' (Mangkunagara 1957, p.18). There he meets a tiny being, *dêwa* Ruci, who is a replica of himself. He enters him and by so doing discovers his spiritual self. The percussion music from the *gamelan* orchestra accompanies Bima throughout his journey, reiterating in its varying rhythms the experience of the *semadi* practitioner in his quest for Perfect Knowledge.

So the court shadow play nowadays, as in the past, crystallises the duty of the rulers, and highlights the qualities which are most prized in particular by the élite, but also respected throughout much of the society - the prime quality being refinement, *kealusan*, which shows itself above all in emotional equanimity, polished behaviour and pleasing appearance. It is, furthermore, unsurprising that the symbolic aspects of the art forms, including the rules of etiquette, became ever more elaborate after the arrival of western influence from the seventeenth century onwards. The Dutch rendered the courts militarily and politically powerless. This lack of political hegemony could, though, to some degree be concealed by the spiritual knowledge the aristocrats were able to acquire through, among other things, the shadow play. As such it emerges that the mythical world represented in the shadow play relates directly to the profane world of experience. It gives a sense of identity to the élite, the *priyayi*, who may use it as a symbol of political power, but also to the peasants already in opposition to the elite.

This is especially true as less philosophically intricate shadow theatre performances are given in the villages in association with rites-of-passage celebrations, or, for example, to counteract illness or to ensure a rich harvest (Brandon 1970, pp.14-16). It is then that it may have a benign influence which has magico-religious overtones. The audience on these occasions comprise primarily the peasant sector of the society, *abangan*, whose religious system is made up of a synthesis of animistic, Hindu and Islam elements (Geertz 1960, p.6).

While the *priyayi* feel a special affinity to the princes and their goals, the peasants have a closer bond to the servants in the shadow play. As one scholar (H. O. 1922, pp.169-72) put it, they are the mouthpiece of the simple village people, of their strength, wisdom and misery. So far the servants have hardly been mentioned, yet they have a crucial role in the play. While rough-looking and ugly, they have great spiritual power. This applies above all to Semar, the senior servant, who on occasions can mediate between gods and men. The servants are not only guardians of their masters, but they are also clowns who frolic around and who are licensed to say things as they really are, exposing if necessary with shrewd rustic wit the flaws in others. In this the servants resemble a figure like Touchstone in *As You Like It*, who is a privileged truthteller and critic.

The proletarian drama, *ludruk*, to which I next wish to turn, belongs to the Little Tradition, being far removed from the sophisticated court form of art, etiquette and philosophical speculations. The main somewhat tangential link that *ludruk* has with the shadow play is via the servants or clowns.

Ludruk is performed throughout east Java, but primarily in the bustling, rather sleazy, port-town of Surabaya, the capital of the province of East Java and one of the most industrialised cities in Indonesia. It has a population of over two million and is composed of several ethnic groups, comprising Europeans, Chinese and Indonesians.

Plays are often given in the village outskirts, *kampung*, as also in the five commercial theatres of Surabaya. The participants – the actors, the managers and the spectators – belong to the proletarian sector of the society, being labourers, builders, road sweepers, artisans, petty traders and clerks. Most of them are poor and ill-educated, having had no more than four years of education. The belief system of the proletarians can loosely be classified as *abangan*, as it is essentially syncretic. Many of the *ludruk* participants in the past were sympathetic to the Communist cause and in 1963 this genre became affiliated with the Communist Party. Since then, however, Suharto has become president and the government keeps a close eye on *ludruk*. This Marxist leaning was mainly evident in the songs about poverty sung by the servants, who represent the archetypal impoverished proletarians. Islamic merchants, the *santri*, seem never to attend *ludruk* as they are shocked by the male transvestites who play female parts; this theatre form is too lewd and garish for them. Members of the élite, who live in the centre of town, also do not watch *ludruk* as they consider it too coarse. Its shabby, lurid atmosphere is of course intensified as prostitutes, gamblers, drunks, beggars and thieves intermingle with the audience.

This theatre genre has been discussed primarily by the anthropologist Peacock (1968), who argues that *ludruk* encourages the modernisation of Javanese society. Javanese proletarians think in terms of two sets of values which are the traditional refined/coarse (*alus/kasar*) opposition, which is also portrayed in the shadow play, and the progressive/conservative, or *maju/kuno*, opposition. As the old patterns change the Javanese are increasingly coming to see their society according to the progressive/conservative distinction and *ludruk*, through its stories, songs, jokes and dances, assists them in this process (Peacock 1968, pp.6-8).

The actors, who are all males in *ludruk*, speak in any language appropriate - Javanese, Indonesian or Madurese (the language of a small island on the northeast coast of Java). The clothes are standard everyday ones. The scenery is drop-and-wing. Performances take place in the evening and last for about three to four hours. The songs and dances, which can be highly evocative, always take place between scenes. The two main characters in *ludruk* are undoubtedly the servant and the transvestite, both of whom may be skilled, compelling actors. The servant wears a simple sarong, or khaki trousers, a plain or chequered coloured shirt, a black cap, and is barefoot. A certain sacred aura is attached to him, vaguely reminiscent of the servants in the shadow play. He stands aloof, and is often wiser then the others, at times mocking their values. The transvestite singer tries to resemble a refined, aristocratic female; his face is heavily made up and is framed by a smooth, thick chignon and he wears a fancy sarong. The net effect, though, is that he looks more like a gaudy tarted-up woman of the streets. However, as with the servants, he may retain a certain sacred quality which is induced by his mixing of female and male categories. It is known that transvestites on some of the Indonesian islands had roles as shamans, priests or mediators, with supernatural power at their disposal (Pigeaud 1938, pp.361-2). In the plays, the transvestites are enticing, mystifying figures who through their association with both refinement and illicit sex arouse fantasies and hidden desires in the male spectators (Peacock 1968, p.204).

The themes of the stories dramatised are the most striking indicator of the modernising effect of *ludruk*. Most of the stories are domestic ones, which centre around marriage or attempted marriage and romance. Plots fall into two sorts: the traditional and the modern, the latter being performed increasingly often. Traditional plots revolve around the refined/coarse distinction. They emphasise the importance of kin ties, especially those between siblings, and between parents and children, in contrast to modern stories focused on sexual attraction and love, which turn on the progressive/ conservative distinction. The former are based on a story, such as Malay Dance, where a proletarian actress runs off with an élite school principal, who leaves behind him a pregnant wife. His parents, however, trace his whereabouts and force him to return home (Peacock 1968, p.106). *First Duty*, on the other hand, illustrates a typical modern plot. An aristocratic army officer meets and falls in love with a pretty village girl during the revolution. After the fighting he returns to Surabaya where he obtains a good job. One day he suddenly comes across his former sweetheart who is selling bananas on the street. After some obstacles relating to the conflict have been overcome, the aristocrat and village girl marry and the story ends happily (Peacock 1968, p.109). As evident from this example, modern plots stress social mobility through marriage. Success here depends on achievement which is generally initiated by sex appeal, and entails a break with one's background. In traditional plots, the emphasis is on status and the maintenance of old kin ties, and the outcome of events is determined by fate.

It is with the poverty-stricken servant that the audience sympathises, identifying his plight with theirs. The servants' jokes turn on mixing refined and coarse categories. So a servant may make fun of the refined etiquette of his élite master when he politely passes coffee to his guests by coarsely saying 'Go on, slurp it up' (Peacock 1968, p.155). In mocking the aristocrat for manners which are of course intrinsic to his class, the servant induces laughter in the audience, which is said to be cathartic. Although Peacock does not explicitly mention this, the spectators through these jokes are also able to reduce the élite to common men like themselves, and hence to break down the rigid status barriers between them. The transvestites, in contrast to the servants, are remote and elusive. Their songs refer to the progressive/ conservative distinction and often have a nationalistic flavour:

Indonesia, all my folk,
Islam, Christian, Buddhist and Hindu,
Come, be together, do not quarrel and argue.
Remember, it is time to progress!
(Peacock 1968, p.175).

It is by their mysterious aura and their sexual appeal –
their big, shaking breasts, their voluptuous bodies and their
wiggling hips – as one informant put it to Peacock – (1968,
p.197), that the singers seduce the spectators to accept new
progressive values which imply thinking in terms of relations
outside the village, in urban society, and following more
rational methods of obtaining one's goal, i.e. achieving one's
ends by satisfactory means, and not simply adhering to traditional customs.

It is evident that Peacock in his analysis of *ludruk* was
influenced by Max Weber, as was Geertz in his discussion of
Javanese art. Both Peacock and Geertz see art as expressing
through their symbolic forms varying configurations of consciousness or patterns of meanings which are derived from
unified conceptual schemes. These are related to different
strata in the society, in a similar way as Weber tied particular social groups with particular forms of religiosity. So
for Geertz the shadow play in Java is a cultivated form of
aristocratic art which is linked to the *priyayi*, the élite in
the society, and it expresses their values. He saw *ludruk*, on
the other hand, as a popular serio-comic drama which appeals
predominantly to an *abangan* audience, who are low-class displaced peasants (Geertz 1960, pp.288-95). *Lukruk* is more than
this for Peacock: through its 'vivid and meaningful symbolic
classifiers' (1969, pp.7-8) it actively moulds the values and
emotions of the proletarian participants in such a manner that
they are prone to act, think and feel in a more modern way
(1969, p.238). However, as we shall see when we look at Bali,
the relationship between the patterns of values, in this case
dramatised through theatre, and the society is complex. One
can perhaps question how much *ludruk* actually encourages
modernisation. Peacock gives little evidence to this effect.
Additionally, most of the spectators are married and in between
the ages of twenty-five and fifty, and thus settled in their
specific life-style with marital responsibilities. Social
mobility and modern ideals are for them dreams to be indulged
in, but which cannot be realised easily. The young, moreover,
are not spectators of *ludruk*; they primarily frequent the
cinemas which show western and modern Indonesian films. More
cautiously, though, it can be said that *ludruk* helps its participants to crystallise and clarify the process of modern-

isation in which they are involved, and so enables them to
come to better terms with it.

BALI

The shadow play, *wayang kulit*, and modern drama, *derama*

Theatre is as significant in Bali as in Java. Geertz has
drawn attention to the royal cremations which he describes as
the 'state ceremonials of classical Bali (which) were meta-
physical theatre: theatre designed to express a view of the
ultimate nature of reality' (1980, p.104). However, the complex symbolism of these splendid ceremonies is lost to most
of the participants. It is nowadays, as presumably in the
past, theatre itself which through its varied stimuli of
colour, costume, movement, voice, speech and music, expresses
to the audience man's conception of himself, his place in the
universe, and in society. As in Java, this applies primarily
to the shadow play which the Balinese always connect with
religion, *agama*. As such it dramatises moral values and ideals
which command special respect in the community as they are
regarded as sacred. In fact, all the villagers that I interviewed stressed its didactic role. The following short poem,
obtained from one informant when questioned on the meaning of
the shadow theatre, illustrates this picturesquely:

> Like the bumble bee who ceaselessly smells the
>   fragrance of the flower,
> Like the stag-beetle who day and night never forgets
>   to smell the putrid and wallows in excretion,
> So too there are good and evil actions.

In line with the above, it is unsurprising that the
puppeteer traditionally was regarded as one of the main
teachers in society, the others being the Brahman priest, the
ruler and the father. Although schools had been set up by the
Dutch throughout the twentieth century and children from
isolated villages have at least four years of schooling, and
there are influxes of tourists each year, the shadow theatre
remains one of the principal recognised vehicles for perpet-
uating and disseminating the classical literature as well as
expressing a cosmology and concomitantly a system of morality.
Drama is also considered to have instructive value, but much
less so than the shadow play.

The main immediate difference between theatre in Java and in
Bali is that the various genres have general significance
common to the whole of society, and the symbolism belongs to

the public domain, the patterns of meaning being widely shared across the island; a genre does not serve a particular group as is the case in Java. In as far as the spectators show a preference, this is based on age and sex. For example, the shadow play is mainly watched by men, and drama by unmarried youths.

In order to understand the place of theatre in Bali, it may be   useful to say a little about the society. The Balinese today comprise a population of over two million. They are a Malayo-Polynesian people who practice a variant form of Hinduism which reached Bali from Java, and ultimately India, over one thousand years ago. The population is concentrated in the fertile south central part of the island which is also considered the heartland of the culture, having been the main area exposed to early Indo-Javanese influences. The peasant economy is based largely on irrigated rice cultivation. Villages tend to be tightly clustered and situated on high ground, surrounded by rice fields. The villages are formally ruled by princes who are members of aristocratic families who claim the status of Ksatriyas. This is one of the ranked descent groups into which Balinese society is stratified, namely Brahmans, Ksatriyas, Wesyas and Sudras - according to an ideology similar to the Indian caste system, with spiritual and temporal power being allocated to the Brahmans and Ksatriyas respectively (1). The three high castes are said to be aristocrats who came over from the last great Javanese kingdom of Majapahit, c. fourteenth century. The Sudras, who are for the most part peasants, comprise over ninety per cent of the population. Their predominance is also reflected in theatre. The majority of the participants are ordinary peasants, though high castes may intermingle with them. So, in contrast to *ludruk*, high castes may enact roles in modern drama; they often play the parts of the Sudra servants, which demand special skill and have an ambiguous status, as was already mentioned to be the case in Java. Balinese theatre is a folk art, performed largely by peasants for peasants, so Javanese consider it rustic by comparison with their theatre. This highlights important differences between the two islands.

The shadow play in Bali never reached the sophistication that it did at the courts of central Java; nor were salvation doctrines dramatised for the élite. The dramatic components, while similar, are simpler. Again most of the stories narrated are adapted from the *Mahabharata*. There are fewer puppets in a collection - about eighty. They are sturdier and closer to life than the highly stylized, often ornate, Javanese puppets. The play takes place in a temporary raised booth usually set up on the village wquare. Theoretically the puppeteer is supposed to be a Brahman, but in fact is most commonly a Sudra. As in Java, he is considered a ritual practitioner.

The main occasion for any dramatic performance is in association with the anniversary of a temple (*odalan*), once every 210 days; and it has been calculated that there are over 20,000 temples in Bali. After such a ceremony it is customary throughout the island to have a form of entertainment for three nights running. The shadow play is often chosen as it is the most revered style of theatre, the stories furthermore being thought suitable as they have ethical content; also it is the cheapest genre. Modern drama is also popular, but more just for its entertainment value, as the stories are romantic and lighthearted. On these occasions it is the temple congregation or village council which hires and pays the expenses of the performance. Some puppeteers have Ksatriyas as their special patrons who call upon them to perform at the court, in general for rites-of-passage. Sudras may also request a puppeteer to give a play in their household. No puppeteer, though, can live off his art, for the shadow play is non-commercial.

The servants in the Balinese shadow theatre have perhaps a still more crucial function than in Java, for they must also act as translators of the epic characters who all speak Old Javanese, *Kawi*, which contains a large number of Sanskrit words; in Java they speak in contemporary, albeit formal, Javanese. Although puppeteers may vary in their fluency, few of the audience understand this archaic speech, which has little affinity with the Balinese language spoken by the villagers. The result of this is that the dialogues of the high-caste characters in the play are reduced in length; the emphasis is on the sub-plots which are improvised and woven around the main plot derived from the epic. The sub-plots are based on daily village life and it is during these that the servants clown and frolic around, telling bawdy jokes, as well as discussing issues which have an instructive element. It is here that they expound on such philosophical concepts as duty, *dharma*, or the law of cause and effect, *karma*. A short speech of one of the servants, taken from a play I attended, is given below as it highlights the sort of moral matters which may arise in the shadow theatre. In this speech, the servant Merdah is reprimanding his old father, Tualèn, who is the equivalent of Semar in Java, for trying to make quick money by pretending to be an indigenous medical practitioner, *balian*, and treating disceases about which he has no knowledge.

Merdah:
If you are not trained, you are pretending to have
a skill you do not possess. This will affect your
karma and retribution will be great. If Father does
not know the manuscripts on medical matters, the
religious incantations, the causes of illness or how
to cure them, and never practises meditation, but asks
money from patients, he is in essence stealing from
them. It is also not proper that you should want to
make a profit from curing them

The plays in which such speeches occur have to be seen
within their cosmological framework for the stage, as in Java,
is thought to mirror the macrocosm. The different categories
of beings, which in Bali are patterned on the caste system,
while including gods and ogres, have each their specific
duty, *dharma*, which they ought to carry out. Ideally Brahmans
should teach and give advice; Ksatriyas should administer; and
the Sudras, who are the peasants, should faithfully serve
their masters. So the shadow play illustrates the place of
the caste system in the cosmos.

Action on the stage is, moreover, linked to appearance and
style of movement. Refined-looking puppets, with light-
coloured skins and almond-shaped eyes, act on the whole
according to their image, as do rough-looking ones. As Geertz
has pointed out in discussing Bali, 'art, religion, and
politesse all exalt the outward, the contrived, the well-
wrought appearance of things' (1966, p.56), and this concept
is brought to the fore in the shadow play where the various
dramatic components all reflect one another. In Bali all
castes formalise their relations by following strict codes of
etiquette. Refinement, which implies to the Balinese sweet-
ness of character, apart from poise and restraint, is an
attribute which, while associated with the high castes, is
sought after by low and high castes alike and is thought to
be attainable by any person. A coarse, uncontrolled villager
is ridiculed and shamed.

It is of interest that when Balinese adults are interviewed
about contemporary drama, they draw attention mainly to its
form and not to its content; in fact they often consider the
stories banal. I shall only make a few comments about drama,
for it is the most popular present-day genre with the young,
but when asked, they stress that its appeal relates to its
being a place where they can meet and flirt with the opposite
sex. Traditionally parents frowned upon public flirtation
and courtship.

Derama, as it is called in Balinese, probably derived from
the English word, takes place in the community pavilion of a
village against drop-and-wing scenery. About ten to fifteen
actors are required who comprise both men and women. A troupe
is usually comprised of Balinese from various areas of the
island. Although this genre is commercial, tickets are cheap,
and most actors depend on other professions for their liveli-
hood. A form of *derama* seems first to have existed in 1965
or 1966 when it was called *derama jangèr*. The term has
political overtones. *Jangèran* means a sick, confused chicken.
This type of theatre was accompanied by loud percussion music
and the stories concerned peasants; intense conflict arose
between them and the high castes, which ended to the detriment
of the latter. *Derama jangèr* was said to mirror the confused,
unstable period just after the coup in 1965 when thousands
of people were killed on both islands.

It is noteworthy that *derama* shows latent proximity to the
shadow play – a fact which is recognised by Balinese. This
comes to the fore in its dramatic structure; each performance
is characterised by a division on the stage bewteen two groups
which, as has been mentioned in connection with the shadow
play, is associated with the cosmic dualities. Tension exists
between the two groups, one of which is clearly nobler and
more refined than the other, and which may lead to battle.
The story ends with the nobler party obtaining its goals. The
aristocrats of each group have their specific male servants
and, as in *ludruk*, a sacred aura clings to them. They stand
outside the main plot and at times they show wisdom and in-
sight. The dress of the actors also reflects the shadow play.
For example, kings wear head-dresses and servants usually wear
short black and white chequered loin cloths similar to those
depicted on puppets. The etiquette adhered to between the
castes is generally as strict as in the shadow play. So
servants on the stage always lower themselves bodily when
addressing their masters, and are careful to use the correct
language level when speaking to them. Sometimes the servants
use Indonesian, but this is primarily when they talk among
  themselves.

The stories are not derived from a fixed repertoire. Most
of them nowadays involve lighthearted romance and end happily
with a prince and princess being united after obstacles have
been overcome, which often entails magic. The actors
improvise extensively on stage. The dialogues of the servants
may contain an instructive element, as evident in such
proverbs as:

Cara katak batan celongkakê.
Like a frog under a coconut shell.

Celabingkah di batan biyu,
Gumi linggah ajak liyu.
Broken tiles beneath a banana tree,
The world is big with much in it.

The first proverb is said of someone who is haughty and
thinks he knows everything. The second implies that there are
many people in the world who are all following different paths.
The speeches of the servants, if they are accomplished actors,
may be sprinkled with proverbs. Those above are well-known
in Bali. During the plays, the characters also comment on
varied contemporary issues such as the number of Chinese
shops in the capital, Denpasar, the increase of motor
bicycles on the roads, the new Javanese songs which have
penetrated the island, the strange dress of some tourists,
and so on.

In reviewing theatre in Java and Bali, it is clear that the
shadow play on both islands is the most conservative, traditional and revered form of theatre. Its mythology, moreover,
links it with the whole Hindu culture of south and south-east
Asia. It presents to the spectators a view of the world which
has cosmological dimensions. The ideal is to live in harmony
with this cosmic-social order. This implies above all
avoiding loss of self-control which leads to disharmony. A
cultured man should be polite, restrained and refined. Change
or reform are not part of the *wayang* world where everything
has its place, which is sacred and fixed. Events during a
play may through magico-religious means affect the world of
profane experience, helping to bring prosperity to the land,
health to an individual member of the household, or harmony
to society. In other words, order on the stage, the microcosm,
may create order in the world of men, the macrocosm.

The Balinese shadow play is perhaps still more conservative
than its counterpart in Java. It is frequently performed
throughout the island, when it is watched primarily by
peasants. Such concepts as the doctrine of *karma* or *dharma*
which, as Weber (1958, pp.118-23) has pointed out in regard
to the Indian caste system, are crucial deterring factors to
change, are often brought up in the plays. As in India there
are of course numerous reasons to account for misfortune
(Sharma 1973, pp.347-64), but the law of *karma* is the one the
people most often fall back on to explain long-term effects.

Although the stories recounted in *derama* are secular and

reflect modern trends it, too, takes place in a cosmological setting. Through its emphasis on outward form, which is relatively static, a certain sense of timelessness is imparted to the plays which implies that change on the whole is undesirable.

Ludruk differs from the other forms of theatre discussed. It is far removed from the classic forms of art, and hardly influenced by them. *Ludruk* undoubtedly clarifies and crystallises the nature of the modernising process to its proletarian sector of East Javanese society, the members of which are often displaced peasants, who are increasingly coming into contact with different ethnic, religious and political groups: Madurese, orthodox Moslems, the army, and so on.

CONCLUSION

Finally, I want to add a note on the interplay between the patterns of meaning expressed by theatre and the material base of the society - in other words the relationship between the symbolic and the technical. In *The Protestant Ethic and the Spirit of Capitalism* Weber writes that the 'Puritan outlook ... favoured the development of rational bourgeois economic life' (1976, p.174). Peacock follows a similar line of argument when he points out that *ludruk* encourages rationalisation and modernisation of Javanese society. Weber, however, recognised that the relationship between the symbolic and techno-social was complex and dynamic and that there was feedback between the spheres. This also comes to the fore in examining Indonesian theatre.

Direct interaction occurs between the audience and the performers during any play, when they exchange ideas with one another. Although the outward form is relatively standardised and the basic plot fixed, the sub-plots are continually improvised. This is especially true of contemporary theatre. Peacock remarks on the extent to which the spectators participate in the show by shouting approval or abuse. The same applies to Balinese drama. It is of further interest to note that the servants are always the first actors on the stage in drama. Through their initial jokes and comments on a variety of issues they test out the atmosphere of the audience, and so they and the actors who follow gain an impression of what stimulates, interests and amuses the spectators of the particular village where they are performing. Even in the shadow play it is important that the puppeteer is in tune with the audience, as they simply walk off if bored.

So a play must be seen as a creative process which on one level involves individuals. At the same time, theatre is the art form in Indonesia which expresses and crystallises most vividly values which are shared to a remarkable degree by both specific social groups and the society as a whole. Its force, particularly in the case of the shadow play, also relies on the fact that it takes place in a traditional cosmological framework which gives meaning and legitimacy to the other dramatic aspects.

NOTE

(1) The Wesyas, according to the classical Indian model, are ideally merchants. In the Balinese shadow play they are classified, however, as followers of the Ksatriyas and they have little individuality. The Wesyas lack of prominence in the plays probably accords to their position in the society. Wesyas in Bali are rarely merchants, but are subsumed effectively under the Ksatriyas whom they assist.

BIBLIOGRAPHY

Anderson, B. *Mythology and the Tolerance of the Javanese*, Cornell University Press, Ithaca, N.Y., 1965.
Brandon, J. R. *On Thrones of Gold*, Harvard University Press, Cambridge, 1970.
Geertz, C. *The Religion of Java*, The Free Press of Glencoe, Ill., 1960.
Geertz, C. *Person, Time and Conduct in Bali: An Essay in Cultural Analysis*, S. E. Asia Prog. Cult. Rep. Ser. 14), Yale University Press, New Haven, 1966.
Geertz, C. *Negara: The Theatre State in Nineteenth Century Bali*, Princeton University Press, Princeton, 1980.
H.O., 'Petroek als vorst' in *Djawa* 2, 1922.
Holt, C. *Art in Indonesia: Continuities and Change*, Cornell University Press, Ithaca, N.Y., 1967.
Mangkunagara VII, *On the Wayang Kulit, Purwa, and its symbolic and Mystical Elements*, (trans. C. Holt), Cornell University Press, Ithaca, N.Y., 1957.
Peacock, J. L. *Rites of Modernization: Symbolic and Social Aspects of Indonesian Proletarian Drama*, The University of Chicago Press, Chicago, London, 1968.

Pigeaud, Th. G. Th. *Javaanse Volksvertoningen: Bijdrage tot de Beschrijving van Land en Volk*, Volkslectuus, Batavia, 1938.

Schrieke, B. *Ruler and Realm in Early Java*, Van Hoeve, The Hague, 1957.

Sharma, U. 'Theodicy and the doctrine of Karma', *Man*, 8, 1973.

Weber, M. *The Religion of China: Confucianism and Taoism*, The Free University Press, Glencoe, Ill., 1951.

Weber, M. *The Religion of India*, (trans. and ed. H. H. Gerth and Don Martindale), The Free Press of Glencoe, Ill., 1958.

Weber, M. *The Protestant Ethic and the Spirit of Capitalism*, Charles Scribner's Sons, N.Y., 1958.

Zoetmulder, P. J. 'The wajang as a philosophical theme', *Indonesia*, vol.12, 1971.

6 Attitudes to the world

MICHAEL LEIFER

Two features have distinguished the international outlook of those Indonesians charged with dealing with the world beyond the bounds of the Republic. One is a sense of paradox which in a way corresponds to that inherent in the Republic's motto 'Unity in Diversity'. The other is an underlying sense of continuity which has been characteristic of Indonesia's international outlook since the 1945–49 period of national revolution. The sources and nature of these features of paradox and continuity will serve as our point of entry to an understanding of Indonesian attitudes to the world.

Indonesia is a new state in the sense that there is no historical antecedent for the contemporary political form which secured international recognition in December 1949. Indonesia does not stand in direct lineal descent to a single historical political centre, but emerged as the territorial beneficiary of the Netherlands East Indies. The state frame to which Indonesia succeeded was a product of Dutch colonial manufacture. It involved an administrative fusion of a distended archipelago over a period of centuries. An element of historical myth based upon island empires, less than coterminous with the modern Republic, must be taken into account in identifying and assessing attitudes to the world. But, central to their formation has been the experience of creating a new state through a national revolution whose impact has remained a living legacy. In other words, the founding moments of the

Republic of Indonesia are not partly-remembered history, but are sustained vividly in the memory of a political generation which has enjoyed a relatively long tenure in high office. Indeed, still in charge of the political fortunes of Indonesia are men who have had direct experience of a tumultuous emancipating process which has dominated their thinking. It has been responsible for a common, if paradoxical, view on the part of those who conduct and influence the country's foreign policy.

Those who sit in government offices in the capital city, Jakarta, look with a central metropolitan perspective on the problems of a fragile archipelago. They share in common the view that, despite having been fully independent since December 1949, Indonesia cannot take its independence for granted. The state is contemplated as intrinsically vulnerable to political disintegration. This view   was engendered by the experience of national revolution, during which the Dutch sought to restore their colonial position in a different political form by exploiting the diverse social identities of the embryonic archipelagic state. Continuing fragility was emphasised after the acquisition of independence by abortive acts of separatism, as well as regional rebellions which attracted external support. Vulnerability is not only a problem of containing a brittle combination of people and territory, but also of coping with external powers able to project their military strength at a distance. Indonesia has long attracted outside interests for two reasons. It has done so for centuries because the archipelago has been a rich store of natural resources. This asset and attraction led to the establishment of colonialism. Secondly the geographic location of Indonesia astride the maritime junctions between the Pacific and Indian Oceans gives it a strategic importance, especially for naval powers.

The sense of vulnerability was reinforced by the conviction that the major powers, which it had been presumed would look on Indonesia's claim to independence with benign regard, were not really interested in its moral case, but were willing to compromise the Republic's interests for the sake of *raison d'état*. During the period of revolution, the ambivalence of the United States towards the Indonesian national cause, and the corresponding cynical conduct of the Soviet Union, were the source of the longstanding Indonesian view that the policies of all external powers should be regarded with deep suspicion. Clandestine support by the United States for regional rebels during the late 1950s confirmed the connection between national weakness and vulnerability, and the predatory disposition of foreign states. Although there is a frequently-held contemporary view that Indonesia's prime external threat is now the People's Republic of China, charged with complicity in the abortive coup of October 1965, so-called international partners are regarded with circumspection. For example, Indonesia, from necessity, enjoys a close economic association with Japan, from which it has benefited greatly. It is however a common opinion that Japan is an exploiting power, however much its present methods may differ from those it used in the early 1940s. As for the United States, it is seen as an unreliable strategic partner, even though its government more than a quarter of a century ago gave up any ideas of conniving at the break up of Indonesia.

Concurrent with an abiding sense of vulnerability, there obtains a countervailing and paradoxical sense of national pride, which expresses itself in a strong measure of regional entitlement. Its source lies in the defeat of the colonial power which had ruled the archipelago for centuries. That victory represented for Indonesians of the revolutionary generation an achievement of their *semangat* or fighting spirit, and has become an intrinsic part of national identity. Indeed, revolutionary achievement still serves as a standard by which Indonesians judge the international standing of other states, especially in South-East Asia, and is the basis of national pride. Other credentials include the fact that Indonesia's population of some 150 million is the fifth largest in the world. Its territory and surrounding waters, joined within the encapsulating framework of an archipelagic principle endorsed by the Third United Nations Conference on the Law of the Sea, make Indonesia the seventh largest state in the world. Its rich natural resources, including oil, liquefied natural gas, bauxite, coal, gold, timber, rubber and sugar, have been mentioned above. In addition, Indonesians take pride in the fact that Bandung in West Java was the venue for the first-ever conference of Asian and African states, and that the Republic was a founding member of the non-aligned movement. All of these credentials underpin the view that Indonesia is a potential major power which, at the very least, is entitled to play the leading role in the management of regional order in South-East Asia. In other words, informed Indonesians believe that their country has the right to promote a structure of regional relationships which will provide for both national security and national ambition.

The second distinguishing feature in Indonesia's international outlook has been the way in which these countervailing attitudes, which express themselves in paradox, have been sustained in essence since independence. Although the actual course of Indonesia's foreign policy lends itself to a periodisation marked by contrasts of political style and external affiliations, a distinctive strain of continuity joins the administrations of President Sukarno and his successor, President Suharto. The conventional view is that they differ radically in every respect, especially foreign policy. It is in the latter dimension that they have been in fact most similar, being concerned with national and territorial integrity, and with trying to ensure that external powers were excluded from a primary role in the management of regional affairs. Underlying such common priorities, which have been expressed in varying ways in great part as a consequence of differences in domestic politics, have been the joined factors of vulnerability and entitlement. Thus paradox and continuity have gone hand in hand in attitudes to the world.

For most of its existence as an independent state, the dominant idiom of Indonesia's foreign policy has been expressed in the formula 'independent and active'. To an informed Indonesian this means more than a neutral or a non-aligned foreign policy. It has been employed to indicate that Indonesia intends to be more than a passive spectator of world events, and wishes to play a positive role in the promotion of international peace and security. Aspiration has never been matched by actual achievement. Indeed, the over-ambitious and revolutionary style of foreign policy which distinguished the Sukarno era between 1959-65 was responsible for a transformation in its practice, if not in all of its priorities, and for Indonesia becoming very much of a passive spectator to dramatic events within South-East Asia. The idiom of an independent and active foreign policy which had been allowed to lapse was reinstated with the political succession of General, later President, Suharto, thus restoring a line of continuity from the period of national revolution.

The formula 'independent and active' arose from an episode in September 1948 when the embryonic Republic had been truncated physically as a result of Dutch military action, with the United States, because of its European priorities, adopting an equivocal position to Indonesia's claim to national independence. At that juncture, the left wing of the nationalist movement sought to promote some form of political association between the Republic and the Soviet Union, ostensibly as a way of securing access to a measure of countervailing power against the Dutch. They were baulked by a seminal statement made by Mohammad Hatta, then concurrently Vice-President and Prime Minister, in which he rejected an opening to the Soviet Union on the grounds that it would compromise the independence of the

beleaguered Republic. Hatta's primary intention then was not
to express the ideal course for Indonesia in a hostile outside
world, but to justify denying the initiative of the nationalist
Left. His object was to overcome opposition to the distinctive
approach to the attainment of independence with which he was
identified. That approach, known as diplomacy, depended on
securing the support of the United States to persuade the
Dutch to concede a genuine independence. In the event, it was
successful. But in September 1948, when unequivocal American
support was not assured, Hatta wished to avoid any external
alignment which might alienate the government in Washington,
whose international outlook was conditioned by Cold War con-
siderations.

Although Hatta's statement of foreign policy priorities had
as its immediate objective to uphold the stratagem of diplomacy, it captured the spirit of Indonesian aspirations. It
not only served the foreign policy requirements of the Republic
before the attainment of full independence, it also expressed
an appropriate course of action for the new state as a recognised member of international society. Indeed, the formulation 'independent and active' struck a popular chord as the
rightful stance for a country which had not only rid itself of
colonial rule but also found itself in a world beset by superpower rivalry and did not wish to be drawn into the bitter
contest between the United States and the Soviet Union. Even
under the Administration of President Suharto, whose informal
alignment with the United States has been conspicuous, the
independent and active formula has remained a prominent ideal,
if expressed mainly in symbolic form. When he was re-elected
for a third term in March 1983, a commitment to such a foreign
policy comprised one of the guidelines of state policy
enunciated before the constitutionally sovereign People's
Consultative Assembly. In this respect, if the idea of an
independent and active foreign policy expressed a desire for
an independence that could not necessarily be taken for
granted, it also has served the useful domestic function of
ensuring, up to a point, that external issues would not become
unduly divisive in internal politics.

One important example of the idiom of foreign policy serving
domestic political purposes has been in connection with Islamic
issues. Although approximately ninety per cent of Indonesia's
population are Muslims in one sense or another, the Republic
is not an Islamic state. In effect, the Republic is not bound
culturally by a single great tradition. The most fundamental
source of national diversity is the communal division between
nominal and orthodox adherents of the Islamic faith, most acute

on the pivotal island of Java which contains approximately two thirds of the country's population. That division had its origins in the arrival and acceptance of Islam in the archipelago from around the fourteenth century. In many parts of East and Central Java, Islam was only superimposed on a syncretic cultural tradition which drew its inspiration from entrenched Hindu-Buddhist beliefs. The uneven impact and degree of penetration of Islam has left a divided cultural legacy which continues to trouble the cohesion of the Indonesian state, some forty years after the proclamation of its independence.

The orthodox adherents of Islam within Indonesia have not accepted their numerical minority position. Their claim to politically endorsed religious primacy has long been a source of contention over the appropriate identity of the state. That claim was denied initially in June 1945, when the future President Sukarno enunciated five principles which have served since as the philosophical bases of the Republic: the *Pancasila*, intended to provide a harmonising frame for Indonesian diversity. One of them, above all, was intended to ensure religious pluralism and tolerance expressed in a belief in a single deity which would in turn permit every Indonesian to 'believe in *his own* particular God'. Concerned lest provision for an Islamic state undermine national unity from the outset, Sukarno sought to exclude its prospect through the medium of a syncretic device designed to provide for all forms of religious expression. Under Sukarno and his successor Suharto, recurrent attempts have been made to define national identity without reference to Islam. That domestic priority has possessed an evident international dimension. A prime concern has been to prevent international issues from being used or exploited either to advance demands presented by Muslim groups within Indonesia, or to enhance the political standing of Islam within the Republic. Although Indonesian governments have been obliged to take a stand on some matters of special interest to their Muslim community, such as the status of Jerusalem, they have been influenced strongly by a conviction that incautious engagement in any international Islamic issue might feed back with adverse consequences into the domestic political process. In other words, successive governments have made conscious attempts to excise a co-religionist dimension from foreign policy because of its perceived threat to national unity. Indeed, Indonesia prefers to keep the Arab-Islamic world at a distance and where engagement does take place, it is on the basis of a common non-alignment, not religious identity.

If the independent and active formula in foreign policy has enjoyed a domestic political function, another formula enunciated in December 1957 was intended to reconcile the vulnerability and sense of entitlement of that central paradox which distinguishes Indonesia's international outlook. In 1957, the very future of Indonesia was in doubt because of the extent of regional dissidence and breakdown of political consensus at the centre. Almost by accident, as a result of deliberations by a committee set up to redefine the maritime boundaries of the Republic, the government promulgated an archipelagic principle concurrent with an extension of territorial waters to a distance of twelve miles. That principle constituted a claim to the same quality of jurisdiction over waters, within joined straight base lines which connected the outermost points of the country's outermost islands, as that which obtained over the territory of the archipelago. The object of the exercise was to command, initially in principle, the maritime interstices and perimeter of the state. It expressed a strategic perspective which has been sustained through periods of domestic political change. It was indicated in Indonesia's successful campaign to incorporate politically the western half of the island of New Guinea which had been part of the Netherlands East Indies, but was retained by the Dutch on the transfer of sovereignty in December 1949. That success occurred in August 1962 at the height of Sukarno's presidency. Over thirteen years later, under the more sober leadership of President Suharto, the eastern half of the island of Timor was annexed by force. East Timor had been a Portuguese possession and therefore excluded from the territorial *raison d'être* of the Republic; namely to incorporate all of the former Netherlands East Indies. However, in April 1974 a military coup in Lisbon led to a liberal Portuguese attitude to decolonisation. Indonesia intervened militarily in East Timor in December 1975 to deny the emergence of an independent state of radical leftist disposition located within its security perimeter. That act of denial and territorial incorporation was brutal and costly for the people of East Timor but it demonstrated the strategic continuity inherent in the archipelago perspective.

Having taken account of paradox and continuity in Indonesia's international outlook, it is appropriate to turn to South-East Asia, where the Republic's foreign policy priorities have been concentrated. As suggested above, informed Indonesians believe that as their country is the largest, the most populous, and the one with the greatest natural wealth in South-East Asia, it has the right to play the leading role in the management of regional order. By this they mean a right to prescribe rules or a code of conduct which will govern the behaviour of regional states in such a way that South-East Asia might become self-regulating. Collateral to such an objective has been a concern to exclude as far as possible the competitive intervention of external powers, who have been deemed responsible for so much of the turbulence which has afflicted South-East Asia since the onset of the transfers of sovereignty after the Second World War.

Indonesia's entry into the business of trying to promote regional order on its own terms began seriously after the political downfall of President Sukarno in 1966 and his succession by General Suharto. The latter at the head of a Western-oriented military establishment undertook an un-precedented involvement in regional cooperation through promoting the Association of South-East Asian Nations (ASEAN) in August 1967. ASEAN's founding members apart from Indonesia were Thailand, Malaysia, Singapore and the Philippines; Brunei joined only in 1984. The initial object of the exercise was to promote regional reconciliation; it was only a year since the end of Indonesia's attempt, through a policy of confrontation, to undermine the Federation of Malaysia (of which Singapore had been a constituent part until August 1965). Tensions had obtained also between Malaysia and the Philippines over the latter's territorial claim to part of Northern Borneo, as well as between Malaysia and Singapore over the circumstances of the island-state's separation from the federation. The initiative for regional reconciliation was possible because the five founding members of ASEAN were joined in a pattern of political conformity based on common conser-vative identities, especially marked in the case of Indonesia after the fall of Sukarno. Regional reconciliation was perceived as directly linked to the promotion of internal political stability among the ASEAN states, in part by denying opportunity for competitive external intervention. Moreover, regional co-operation was regarded as a means whereby member countries could give greater attention to their own internal economic development to domestic political advantage. As a long-term aspiration, the ASEAN states affirmed that they shared a primary responsibility for strengthening the economic and social stability of the region, ensuring its countries peaceful and progressive national development, and that they were determined to protect their stability and security from external interference in any form or manifestation. It is of interest to note that such views had been an intrinsic part of the foreign policy goals of President Sukarno's Indonesia and have been sustained not only by President Suharto's admin-istration but also adopted by the Republic's new found regional partners.

By coincidence, shortly after the formation of ASEAN, the balance of external influences bearing on South-East Asia began to change. The British Government announced an accelerated military withdrawal from east of Suez in January 1968. In the following March, the Soviet Union deployed a naval flotilla into the Indian Ocean for the first time. The same month, President Johnson began the agonising reappraisal of American policy in Indochina expressed in turn and more acutely in the enunciation of the Guam Doctrine by President Nixon in July 1969, who went on to make his historic visit to China in February 1972. In such changing circumstances, ASEAN governments became obliged to give more direct attention to problems of regional order, even though collectively they did not dispose of much military capability.

Indeed one member state, Malaysia, undertook a unilateral initiative which gave rise to tensions with its regional partners, especially Indonesia. The Malaysian Government proposed in September 1970 that the whole of South-East Asia become a neutralised zone whose status would be guaranteed by the external powers; namely, the United States, the Soviet Union and China. The Indonesian Government, in particular, took objection to this suggestion because of a conviction that any such system of neutralisation would be equivalent to according virtual policing rights to the external powers and to denying the resident states their entitlement to manage their own affairs. Chinese participation was viewed with considerable apprehension in the light of the strong consensus within Indonesia's military establishment that the People's Republic posed the principal long-term threat to the security of the Republic. Indeed, it was primarily as a result of Indonesian initiative at a meeting of ASEAN's foreign ministers in November 1971 that the principle of neutralisation was deliberately diluted. The five governments committed themselves to an alternative, much vaguer, aspiration for the establishment of a Zone of Peace, Freedom and Neutrality. That formula expressed Indonesia's approach to regional order; namely, that there should be a co-operating system of resident states who through their own efforts would seek to manage international relations within South-East Asia and in the process insulate it from the unwarranted intervening activities of external powers. Although Indonesia was obliged to watch the dramatic success of revolutionary communism in Indochina in 1975 from the sidelines, it sustained its regional vision. At the first-ever meeting of ASEAN heads of government which convened on the island of Bali in February 1976, a Treaty of

Amity and Co-operation was concluded which expressed
Indonesia's priorities for regional order in the form of an
inter-state code of conduct. This treaty, which affirmed
respect for national sovereignty, made provision for adherence
by regional states beyond the ASEAN structure. In other words,
it was intended as a bridge to the Communist states of
Indochina.

Subsequent regional events have served to deny Indonesia's
regional vision and also to expose a deep and abiding sense of
frustration over its inability to play a full managerial role.
When Vietnam invaded and occupied Kampuchea from December
1978, it violated the cardinal rule of the international
system of states. It despatched its army across an internationally recognised political boundary, removed the government of a neighbouring state, and replaced it with an administration of its own choice. Despite the bestial record of the
ousted Pol Pot regime, Indonesia took exception to that
action, in part because it had violated the spirit of ASEAN's
Treaty of Amity and Co-operation. Vietnam's military intervention generated a sense of apprehension because if its
violation of national sovereignty were to be endorsed, then a
very unhealthy precedent for political change would be
established. Indonesia's public opposition to Vietnam was
governed also and importantly by the reaction of its regional
partner, Thailand, towards whom it was obliged to display
intra-ASEAN solidarity.

For Thailand, Vietnam's invasion of Kampuchea constituted a
violation of strategic environment. Its action marked an un-
precedented historical situation in terms of the territorial
projection of Vietnamese power to its borders. It gave rise
to a concern that a new concentration of power might emerge in
mainland South-East Asia, to which Thailand might stand in a
similar subordinate way as Finland to the Soviet Union. For
that reason, and because there was a military force in the
form of the Khmer Rouge prepared to challenge Vietnam's
occupation, and more importantly because of China's deter-
mination not to tolerate the new *status quo*, Thailand was
prepared to confront the government in Hanoi. Moreover, it
insisted that its regional partners stand by it as a front-
line state in opposing Vietnam's occupation, and in demanding
the restoration of Kampuchea as a buffer state interposed
between Vietnamese power and Thailand's vulnerability.

The problem for Indonesia in this exercise in the regional
balance of power is that it has found itself drawn into a
coalition of states with China. Indeed, a tacit alliance

relationship has developed between Thailand and China, while the latter serves as the foundation stone of a strategy of attrition which is designed to place a breaking strain on the society and government of Vietnam. Such a strategy is innately distasteful to Indonesia, because Vietnam is regarded as more nationalist than communist, and a natural partner in obstructing the expansion of Chinese influence.

While Indonesia supports Thailand in terms of principle and also understands its strategic priorities, it is profoundly concerned lest the consequences of the strategy of attrition lead to one of possibly two objectionable outcomes. The first would be the political breakdown of a debilitated Vietnam subject to Chinese influence, which would then have open access to the rest of South-East Asia. The second would be a broken-backed Vietnam, sustained through a relationship of undue dependence on the Soviet Union, which in turn would have a consolidated military reach within South-East Asia. These are prospects which the Indonesian government finds very disturbing, but it cannot do much to resolve the Kampuchean conflict. For example, if it were to break ranks with ASEAN, it would not be likely to affect the tacit alliance between Thailand and China. Indeed, it might only reinforce it and so Indonesia could lose all its political capital invested in ASEAN since 1967. Moreover, that would not alter relations between Vietnam and the Soviet Union.

For the time being, at least in respect of Indochina, Indonesia has not been able to pursue an independent and active foreign policy. It tends to be more of a spectator than an actor and its present government is obliged to contain its frustration, up to a point, because ASEAN is regarded still as the cornerstone of its foreign policy. Accordingly it has to stand by Thailand and wait until changes in the balance of contending forces in Indochina either lead to the success of the policy to which Thailand and its regional partners are committed, or until a need arises to accommodate to new circumstances which Thailand will have to accept. This is an ironic circumstance, in the sense that Indonesia has become the captive of its own creation. President Suharto made it known in a speech in 1968 that Indonesia was the primary force in the establishment of ASEAN. Now the very viability and resilience of ASEAN serves as a constraint on a foreign policy that in official formulation is known still as independent and active.

Indonesia's attitudes to the world have not changed in any fundamental sense but they constitute an expression of aspirations and not achievement. Those attitudes can only remain at the level of aspiration because national weakness, especially in economic terms, has not been overcome in a way that permits Indonesia to assume a commanding role as manager of regional order.

Further reading

In addition to the books on Indonesia mentioned above, the following, currently in print, may be found of interest.

Aveling, H. (ed), Development of Indonesian Society, University of Queensland Press, St Lucia 1979.
Crouch, H., Army and Politics in Indonesia, Cornell University Press, Ithaca 1978.
Higgins, B., Indonesia's Economic Stabilisation and Development, n.e., Greenwood Press, London 1982.
Legge, J.D., Indonesia, Prentice-Hall, Sydney 1981.
Ricklefs, M., History of Modern Indonesia, Macmillan London 1981.
Wertheim, W.F., Indonesian Society in Transition: a Study in Social Change, Greenwood Press, London 1980.

Further Reading